6 VOCATIONAL PERSPECTIVES SERIES

Poverty:

sign of our times

aloysius Schwartz

alba house
DIVISION OF THE SOCIETY OF ST. PAUL
STATEN ISLAND, N.Y. 10314

Nihil Obstat:
Edward Higgins, O.F.M. Cap.
Censor Librorum

Imprimatur:
Joseph P. O'Brien, S.T.D.
Vicar General, Archdiocese of New York
October 11, 1969

The nihil obstat and imprimatur are official declarations that a book or pamphlet
is free of doctrinal or moral error. No implication is contained therein that those who
have granted the nihil obstat and imprimatur agree with the contents, opinions or
statements expressed.

Library of Congress Catalog Card Number: 79-109384

Designed, printed and bound in the U.S.A. by the Pauline Fathers and Brothers,
2187 Victory Blvd., Staten Island, N.Y. 10314 as part of their communications
apostolate.

SBN: 8189-0169-1

"What did you go out to the desert to see? A reed shaken by the wind? But what did you go out to see? A man clothed in soft garments? Behold, those who wear fine clothes and live in luxury are in the houses of kings."

Luke 7, 24-26

Table of Contents

Introduction

By Monsignor John Zeder

They were five minutes too late. In that brief time I turned to the back cover of *America Magazine* through which I had been thumbing. There an ad started with the bold headline "HELP US!" It went on to touch upon some of the very restlessness that had been surging through my own priesthood. The poor; the call to serve the poor; the undeveloped nations. How can the Church come into the lives of the poor? How does a priest-principal such as myself secure in his little apostolate in an up-state New York high school, get involved?

It caused no immediate drama that night. I didn't walk out on the parents group gathering in the school library. Nor sell my Plymouth. But it was one more link in a long chain of events that slowly brought about just such a change. It also paved the way for meeting the author of this book.

Ten months later I listened to this book being born. Hunched up on a sleeping mat on the cold, concrete floor of a small Korean office, three of us listened as Father Schwartz read some of its opening pages. In the meantime I had talked with Father Schwartz in our faculty residence in that up-state New York village. I had walked with him through slums in Pusan, Rio de Janeiro, Caracas, and Lima. My Plymouth was gone; and I had walked away from that school. I didn't agree with all that I heard on those first few pages. I still don't agree with all that is in this finished version. But I better understand the fire that seems to burn just behind the words.

That's the trouble with the Church of the Poor. It upsets you. It makes demands of you that upset a lifetime of values. Of all of the statements developed in this book the one verified most by my own experience is that you can't understand the Church of the Poor while living in a middle class environment. The pleasantness of the life muffles the urgency. But there is an urgency. It breaks through every page of this book, just as it broke through the stately prose of the Encyclical *On the Developing Nations*. Gone was the quiet serenity of Pope Paul when he wrote, "We have desired to remind all men how crucial is the present moment, how urgent the work to be done. The hour for action has sounded."

Aloysius Schwartz is no Pope Paul. He is not always a serene man. His main resemblance to the Holy Father is a similar slightness of stature. Not that he is a frail man. The commitment to the poor that fires his words also sparks his slight frame. Slimmed by endless activity and a no nonsense diet, he seems to mirror that constantly driving energy that is the mark of the Korean people among whom he lives.

This energy has driven him into some strange circumstances. His studies for the priesthood began conventionally enough, enrolling in St. Charles Minor Seminary in Baltimore. Then, College and Philosophy with Maryknoll at Glen Ellyn, and finally, theology at Louvain with the Samists. One summer in Paris with Abbé Pierre, another in a little clinic in the Sahara Desert during the Moroccan uprising. Finally, ordination in Washington, D.C. and incardination in the diocese of Pusan, Korea. Those who finish this book will catch other little autobiographical glimpses of him moving out of his Korean rectory into a poor man's shack, or beginning a community of Korean Sisters dedicated to the poor and the witnessing of poverty.

There is one aspect of the author that doesn't come through

the words of this book. I suppose that is the price of assuming the prophet's role. I am afraid that our image of prophets still evokes pictures of deserts, burning sun, and the voice of one calling in the wilderness.

But a prophet today, like Jonah of old, wearies of his burden. He slips off the prophetic role on a hot day to dive into the near-by sea, testing the strength of his arms against the ebb of the tide, startling an ancient Korean fisherman who discovers a "round eyed" westerner bobbing in the middle of his bay. He plans picnics for young Korean aspirants to the religious life along the gentle, terraced hills of the "Land of the Morning Calm." In his daily work he bends down to comfort a tearful orphan, stops in his weary climb through the muddy slums to console a mourning widow. And like the Psalmist, he finds the time in a hectic sched-ule to walk across the hills where mountain meets the sea and to behold the glory of God shining out of all his creation. Then he stands on those same hills, sees teeming slums with their wretched poor walled in by the indifference of millions, and cries over the New Jerusalem that seems so delayed in coming. You will hear some of those cries on the pages that follow. I could only tell you of the tender love of the poor that wrings those cries out of a compassionate heart.

There are other facets of Father Schwartz's personality that evade his own writing. A dreamer, yes; an idealist, yes. But a terrible realist as well. As he himself writes, "The response to poverty has to be more than a pity, a sorrow. It has to involve bringing an effective response to the needs of the poor." Whether it be through the small family-styled approach for bringing care to the orphans, self-help programs for slum families, or a highly successful fund raising program, he has left a definite mark on social programs throughout all of South Korea.

I hope that I will be excused for enlarging a bit on one phase of the work of Father Schwartz even though I am personally involved in it. This has to do with his efforts to form a new mission group guided by the principles of Vatican II. As a result of his reflections over the years he earnestly believed that there was a need for another mission sending group; one which is diocesan in spirit, dedicated to the urban poor and the witnessing of the poor Christ. This was the reason for the ad that served as my own introduction to the Church of the Poor. It echoed that cry for help rising up from the millions of the poor scattered throughout the world. It is a cry that too often falls upon deaf ears.

Christ chose a role of poverty, then pointed to himself as the Way. Through the years there has been a constancy in the saints' desire to imitate this way of Christ. It is terribly wrapped up in the whole of His calling. To leave all things; to sacrifice all things; to come follow Him.

This is especially true for working among the poor. We can justify our detachment all we want in the name of the spirit of poverty, yet it remains true that souls go unserved with increasing frequency because we will not pay the cost of working among them. As our own standard of life becomes more enriched, it becomes increasingly harder to leave all things. Like the young man in the Gospel, we go away sadly because we have many possessions.

In that happy frankness found in discussions among priest friends, how rarely is some hoped-for assignment discussed in the terms of service. Where can I best serve the lowly, the neglected, the outcasts? We do not hear it often. Instead, with that frailty that we priests share with the rest of humanity, the new assignment is discussed in terms of how it might relate to the conditions of our personal lives. "It is good parish." But what do we mean? The quality of the buildings? The niceness of the people? The comfort of the living? These all too human values are much, much too present in our priesthood.

I have just been reading through the Epistles of St. Paul. They never fail to disturb me. How they cry out with the suffering he found in his service of Christ. It was Paul's joy, and his agony. But how calmly he expected it. Like master, like disciple. There had to be a cross in his priesthood.

Heaven forbid that our priesthood is going soft. But it will reflect our culture. It is harder to follow Him all the way. We don't quite trust Him to take care of us. After all, the Christian joy that begins to abound again in our day cannot be a joy based on non-suffering. Not if it is the joy of Christ. There has to be a cross in it; with real pain, real nails; and a few real welts raised on our backs. The joy of the Christian is one that sees through the suffering to the resurrection.

At least that part of Father Schwartz's dream has begun to be realized. That mission group has been formed. It is called Vatican II International Mission Service. We're just a handful, sort of a preface of things to come. A group of priests banded together by the common ideals of serving the poor, giving witness to the poorness chosen by Christ, and striving to build up in the Church a greater awareness of her call to seek out the poor and lowly, and go comfort them.

We have a long way to go, with many programs to explore and, undoubtedly, many mistakes to make. Perhaps in total numbers we will never become a significant influence in the Church. But in the meantime, some of the poor are being served, and we grow a little more each day in our following of Christ.

In his first book, *The Starved and the Silent,* the author stirred up discussion among the missionary communities of Korea. Not all of it was pleasant. This book is bound to be equally controversial. Maybe it should be. Maybe that is a sign of a healthy rebirth. Time was when we didn't talk about poverty; at least not with a fiery conviction. We had come to terms with it by fashioning a convenient compromise to the urgings of Christ. Christians, and especially Christian religious, had evoked a non-personalized collectivism that seemed to safeguard the call to detachment without unduly taxing our belief in the providence of the Father. Security and a full life seemed to be more a problem of selecting competent administrators than in confidently casting ourselves upon the providence of God.

Occasionally real poverty did enter religious life. Yet even then it assumed more the aspect of a tragedy than a triumph. A fire, a loss, a persecution and we quickly gave evidence that our detachment wasn't real, just de-personalized. We might sacrifice the "my" but God help those who threatened "ours." Even the contradictory example of our saints more often constituted an ornamental testimony to the rightness of our values than a spur to imitate the hardness of their lives. A sort of vicarious sanctity emerged that established the validity of our calling without unduly hampering our comfort.

I find it harder to analyze the poverty in the diocesan priesthood. Perhaps it is too fragmented. Sharing in the social inequities around them, some priests suffer while other abound in luxury. I don't know all the facts. I only know certain American priests. In these times, in this country, I do not know a priest who is a poor man. Not one. Maybe I have been too shielded. But then, maybe they have become too few. At a time when so few of us American priests have to be poor by circumstances, it would seem fitting for more of us to choose to be poor by conviction. Like Christ. Anyhow, that, in part, is what this book is about.

It's about a kingdom too. A kingdom not of this world. "My kingdom is not of this world" Christ told Pilate, but then what are we doing with "Princes of the Church," "Episcopal Palaces," and "Chanceries." Even our speech betrays us. It is not the function of governing God's people that is contrary to Christ's spirit. It's the style of that governing. Where is the servant-Church? The embracing of the poor? I dare say we have given more banquets for the princes of this world than we have for the poor.

Tragically, this applies to liturgical feasting as well. The powerful, the rich, and the prominent of this world have not suffered from a lack of spiritual ministration. Nor have their children. They still receive the best of our education, the best of our healing, the best of our concern. We are with them, and we serve them. And in those disturbing moments of real honesty, we prefer it that way. But is it Christian?

A chapter in this book makes much of the inequitable distribution of material wealth. In this world 15 per cent of the people have 85 per cent of the wealth. That shocks us. It doesn't unduly disturb us though, as long as we are among that happy 15 per cent. But the distribution of the spiritual resources too often reflects that same inequity. That same 15 per cent of souls has the benefit of nearly the same 85 per cent of priests and sisters. The "have not" nations too often are the spiritual "have not's" as well. Calling the poor "the preferred children of the kingdom of God" is not a catch phrase coined by the author. It is the salutation solemnly bestowed upon them by the Fathers of the Second Vatican Council. And it is a reminder to everyone entrusted with reevaluating the direction of traditional apostolates in this age of renewal. This too is what the book is about.

I'm sure this isn't to be the last word on poverty, the poor, and serving them. What Father Schwartz writes about is his beginning. Like the rest of us, his judgments are colored by his experiences. They are Korean experiences. The experience of poverty, real poverty; with pinched faces, swollen joints, and glazed stares. The experience of the incongruity of religious poverty in an undeveloped nation where embracing the vow of poverty means an improvement in every aspect of your physical life. The experience of missionary activity that too often has replaced the flag of nationalism that used to fly over Catholic mission compounds with the flag of richness, bigness and gadgets.

Already this introduction has grown too long. I had better let you read the book for yourself. I hope you like it. I myself still fight parts of it. And I always will. Some of that is my fault. Some of that is the fault of the author. But a lot of it is the fault of Christ. He preached a compelling message, in words and example. We can try to ferret out the chaff that human frailty has added to that Christ-call. But we must go slowly. He called for a radical overturning of standards and judgments. A kingdom of the lowly and poor that still is laboring to be born. When we hear Him, we still run scared — not quite believing.

Monsignor John Zeder

CHAPTER I

A Gentle Warning

Right here, in the opening chapter, I wish to put the reader on his guard. The subject of poverty is a dangerous one. It is quite capable of stirring up violent emotion in the hearts of people of otherwise perfectly meek and humble temperament.

There is no problem with spiritual poverty. Everyone is agreed — and always has been, I guess — that this is a good thing. But as soon as you begin writing about material poverty, it is a different story. People will feel directly and personally threatened by your words. Subsequently, a type of defense mechanism will be called into play which is capable of dispensing a million and one rationalizations to justify any position one wishes to take on the subject.

Some of these rationalizations are subtle and, at times, very difficult to refute. Others are more simplistic, and still others are just downright silly. Let me give an example or two of what I mean.

While in the United States recently I had occasion to stay overnight in a brand-new $200,000 rectory in a large suburban parish. The rectory was unusually plush and among many re-markable features, boasted a fountain with running water in the living room and exquisite oakwood panelling throughout. The pastor patiently explained to me the advantages of oakwood over Kemtone or wall paper which ordinary people are accustomed to use in their ordinary houses. The fact seems to be that Kemtone or wall paper need frequent re-doing, which of course is costly. Such is not the case with oakwood; a hundred years hence and it will still be standing — un-repaired and un-retouched — in all its pristine splendor. Pursuing this line of reasoning to its logical conclusion, it can be stated that the choice of oakwood panelling was made in the spirit of pastoral economy.

As for the living room fountain with the running water, that too can be explained. The pastor put it to me this way: "You've got to realize, Father, that a priest doesn't build a rectory for himself. It's for the people, and the people of my parish at least don't want their pastor living in squalor."

Another similar tongue-in-cheek example comes to mind. This one concerns a priest acquaintance of mine whom I shall refer to as Father Placidus. Since Father Placidus is associate pastor in a large parish his priestly duties among other things include many sick calls. Recently, Father Placidus traded in his old model Ford for a brand new fire-engine red hard top convertible. When some of the people of the parish wondered out loud whether the car wasn't a bit too flashy for a priest, Father Placidus was heard to reply: "Why, I bought it to use on my sick calls; and when you think of it, really, nothing is too good for the Blessed Sacrament!"

Another phenomenon related to poverty which never ceases to amaze me also is how everyone is prone to talk poor-mouth. For some odd reason no one is willing to admit that he is rich, well-off or, for that matter, just plain comfortable. The well-fed seminarian in his plush upper middle class seminary thinks he is leading a life of simplicity. The bishop who lives like a millionaire will tell you how much of a pauper he is and how much he is to be pitied because his diocese is thirteen million dollars in debt. The pastor who has just returned from a $1,500 vacation in Europe is convinced that his style of living is just one degree removed from downright destitution. And to complete the series, the Catholic parent will go on and on describing his struggle to make ends meet on a pittance salary of a mere $10,000 a year. Trying to get anyone to concede that, compared to the rest of the world at least, he is rich, is like trying to get him to admit that he wears a wig or dyes his hair. In this context, one is reminded of the words of Leon Bloy who once said: "I cried because I had no shoes — until I met a man who had no feet."

If rationalizations abound, objections to material-poverty-virtue are in no way lacking either. They range from the *reductio ad absurdum* ("Christ didn't walk the streets of Jerusalem naked, did he?"); to the more subtle intellectual objection ("It's ridiculous to say Christ indwells the person of the poor because by relieving the poor of his poverty you would at the same time be divesting him of his essential dignity").

Also, the argument *ad hominem* is frequently used to good advantage against anyone who descends from the clouds and attempts to write everyday words on the subject of material poverty. Such a person automatically leaves himself open to the charge of pride, self-righteousness, and holier-than-thouism. And, of course, he is always lacking in charity. All of which may not be false. But just as there are many types of poverty, e.g., spiritual, material, economic, and religious, so, too, there are many forms of charity — one which is criticism which is candid and constructive.

Suppose, for instance, that one were asleep in a crowded room and awoke in the middle of the night to find it filled with lethal gas. What would be the charitable thing to do? The charitable, and really constructive thing to do would be to grab a chair and start smashing windows. Others in the room who were asleep or who, although awake, could detect no gas, would take a dim view of the window-smasher's activity. Nonetheless, the window-smasher, according to his own light and conviction, would be performing a constructive act and would be expressing, in an authentic manner, love for his fellow man.

Recently, a well-known and well-revered Church prelate issued a public statement in which he declared it intolerable for the people of God to criticize the Church openly. This is one school of thought; it is not the only one. In the tradition of the Church, one sees that there are saints who criticized and saints who did not. It is difficult to say whether one group is holier or better than the other. One is also reminded of the example of Christ himself. He severely and publicly criticized the established church of his day — not in order to destroy it but to perfect it. Another example which comes to mind is that of St. John the Evangelist. In the Apocalypse, St. John takes to task, in public for all time, four of the seven churches of Asia Minor.

There is no gainsaying the power of public opinion when effectively brought to bear on an issue which should be re-thought, and, possibly, reformed. It is a pressure infinitely greater than the sum of its parts. What is more, it is *sui generis* and often the only pressure which one without juridical authority can bring to bear on a given situation. People in places high and low are extremely sensitive to the full glare of publicity, and will sit up and take notice when it is directed at them. Granted it is a pressure at times difficult to control; nonetheless, it can be converted into a constructive channel of charity.

Vatican II announced a new Pentecost for the Church and called for renewal, reform, and change. The renewal which is to take place in the Church must center on poverty and service of the poor otherwise it will be irrelevant and unauthentic. Unless the people of God quickly become aware of this, the "New Pentecost" will simply remain a catchphrase, and words like "aggiornamento" will remain empty slogans.

What is more, time is running out. It has been said that the Church required a hundred years to implement the decrees enacted at the Council of Trent. We don't have a hundred years today. At most we have, perhaps, ten. We are the "where-the-action-is" people and ours is the "now generation," the "instant society." The pace of living has accelerated to such a dizzying degree that five years today is roughly equivalent to fifty years several centuries ago. There is a sense of urgency in the air, then, which makes the problem all the more acute.

St. Paul, in his Epistle to the Corinthians, writes that the night has passed and the dawn is at hand. In the light of the new dawn, which the Vatican Council ushered in, the virtue of poverty takes on special significance and the poor of the world are seen to be signs of salvation to be accepted or rejected.

CHAPTER II

Poverty: Sign of the Times

"Sign of the times" is an expression which is very much in vogue today. The late Pope John used it frequently, and the Council Fathers in turn adopted it as their own. It is also a gospel expression heard on the lips of Christ himself. What precisely does it mean?

"Sign of the times" may be described as the sum total of events, circumstances, and words which indicate the will of God for the people of God at a given time in history. In this sense, it can be said that poverty — the twofold virtue of material poverty and service of the poor — is a sign of the times today and in a special way the will of God for our generation. Today, it seems that the Spirit of God is moving the people of God towards a new and totally fresh awareness of this often overlooked Chistian virtue and gospel value.

Such a thesis, of course, cannot be proved mathematically as two and two are four; nevertheless, there are strong indications both within the Church and within society that this is so. Moreover, the Church herself has repeatedly spoken out on the issue both individually and collectively, both prophetically and hierarchically.

Before and during the Council there were many individual prophets of this so-called "new" poverty. Pope John is perhaps the most famous of these. In this oft-quoted September 1962 address, he declared: "The Church of Jesus Christ is the Church of all, but especially the Church of the poor." The expression "Church of the poor" marvelously caught the temper of the times and became the battle cry of a new breed of Christians.

In the same vein, Pope Paul VI, in his last pastoral letter as Archbishop of Milan, wrote: "Poverty is the robe of Christ and of his followers who want to imitate, represent, and preach him. The poor are first in the kingdom of God. The society born from Christ will be founded not on luxury, power, or trust in temporal goods, but on the empty terrain of poverty which is supported by a virtue that is wholly spiritual and helped and sustained from heaven. This is the economy of the gospel perpetuated in *Ecclesia Pauperum,* the Church of the poor. John XXIII has proposed that the Ecumenical Council should take this theme for its meditation and reform."

Cardinal Lercaro, in a forceful intervention during the first session of Vatican II, stated: "My intention is to make us more attentive to that aspect of the mystery of Christ in the Church which is of the greatest historical timeliness. I mean, the mystery of Christ in the poor.

"We shall not be doing our tasks well unless we make the mystery of Christ in the poor and the preaching of the gospel to the poor the heart and center of our work at this Council.

"If we treat this subject as just another of the many themes which must occupy the attention of the Council, we shall not satisfy the most profound need of our day.

"In its future deliberations, let the Council give not merely some attention but pride of place to the development of the Gospel doctrine of the holy poverty of Christ in the Church. In particular, it should clarify God's design in choosing poverty as the sign and form of the presence and saving grace of the Word made flesh among men."

Archbishop Helder Camara of Recife, Brazil, sent a letter to his fellow-bishops at the Council which began with a quotation borrowed from St. John Chrysostom: "How can we squander money on construction of temples of stone while we forget the living Christ present in the person of the poor?" Bishop Camara then went on to write: "Let us have the courage to re-examine our conscience and manner of life. Have we adopted the capitalist mentality, methods, and practices which would fit bankers very well but which, perhaps, are not very appropriate in one who is another Christ? May we not be accused, before the Supreme Judge of capitalism, of connivance, or lack of integrity because of the alms we have received? It is said of St. Francis of Paola that when he received gold coins from the king of Naples, who was guilty of usury and injustice, he broke one of the coins and blood flowed from it. May there not be sweat and blood in the alms we receive? Then let us have the courage to admit that the splendor of the Vatican is a great stone of scandal to be removed from our path. Providence has already freed us of the papal states. When will the hour of God sound forth that will bring the Church of Christ to meet Lady Poverty again?"

Bishop Mercier of the Sahara in North Africa spoke as follows: "Each generation brings to the Church its own special, spiritual contribution. What a blessing it would be if it should prove to be the privilege of the twentieth century to enrich the Church with the doctrine of Christ's presence among the poor as the Middle Ages enriched her with the doctrine of his eucharistic presence. On the whole, the Christian world is materially rich. It would find in this doctrine a powerful stimulus to deliver the non-Christian world from its misery, from its crushing burden of poverty. The Church today is afraid of losing the under-privileged countries as, in the past, she lost the working class of Europe. The salvation of this great mass of humanity depends on the stimulus of this doctrine — a doctrine to which, especially, the laity must respond."

Bishop Ancel of Lyon said: "We find ourselves at the beginning of a new era in the history of the Church. John XXIII did not hesitate to say that the Council would be a new Pentecost for the entire Church. Especially in what concerns poverty, we are convinced that an irresistible movement has been launched. This is all the more reason for us to commit ourselves with courage and wisdom."

Cardinal Leger, the former Archbishop of Montreal, in a statement issued on November 9, 1967 said: "The Church is, therefore, essentially a missionary body. The day when she ceases to go toward those who have not yet received the Gospel, she will have become a ghetto and will have been unfaithful to her mission. But if the Gospel must be proclaimed to all men, it is directed first of all to the humble, to the poor in spirit for whom our Lord always showed a particular concern."

These are but a few examples of words being spoken and written today on the subject of voluntary poverty and service of the poor. In passing, it may be well to touch on the personal credentials of those cited above in order to establish their authenticity.

Pope John caught the imagination of the world by his spirit of poverty and the warmth and simplicity of his style. Pope Paul in turn impresses people by the sincerity of his efforts in behalf of world peace and the world's poor. These two are well known and need little mention.

Cardinal Lercaro, as once Bishop of Bologna, opened his episcopal residence to receive poor university students with whom he continues to share his quarters and his table. Archbishop Helder Camara of Recife, Brazil, is a very controversial figure; however, there is a certain charismatic, prophetic quality about the man which can not be ignored. His diocese is located in one of the most economically depressed areas in the world, and his efforts in behalf of social justice have stirred up vitriolic opposition on the part of some politicians and wealthy landowners. Bishop Camara himself just recently moved out of his episcopal palace and took up residence in a refurbished one-room sacristy. Bishop Mercier's diocese is in North Africa and includes part of the Sahara Desert. Enroute to the Council, the Bishop landed at Genoa and walked the distance to Rome begging for his food and keep. Once when he could find no other place to stay he spent the night under a bridge. Bishop Ancel, auxiliary bishop of Lyon, is also Superior General of the Priests of Prado — a society of diocesan priests dedicated in a special way to poverty and service of the poor. For a number of years, Bishop Ancel has worked as a shoemaker and enjoyed the unique distinction of being a "worker-bishop." Cardinal Leger left Montreal for Africa in December 1967; he is now working as a simple missioner in a leper colony in the Cameroons.

Mention should be made here also of the so-called "Church of the Poor" group which was organized within the heart of the Council itself to study the problem of poverty and service of the poor. The group met at regular intervals at the Belgian College in Rome and exerted a real, although limited, influence on shaping Council doctrine. Members of the group included Cardinal Gelier, Father Gauthier, the French worker-priest from Nazareth, Father Yves Congar, the Dominican author of *Power and Poverty in the Church,* and Father François Houtart, the well-known sociologist from Louvain.

Along somewhat similar lines, a small group of bishops— many of whom were members of the Church of the Poor group —met at the close of the Council in a small chapel of the catacombs. After offering Mass together, they pledged themselves, in a special and solemn manner, to imitate Christ in his poverty and service of the poor.

Further proof that poverty is a sign of the times can be seen in the several encyclicals issued before, during, and after the Council. Among these are *Pacem in Terris, Mater et Magistra,* and *Progressio Populorum,* all of which deal in some form or another with poverty and service. In the last mentioned document, *Progressio Populorum,* Pope Paul does a rather unusual thing for an official encyclical he cites a priest by name. The priest in question, although certainly renowned for holiness, has as yet been neither canonized nor beatified. He is, however, an inspiring example of poverty and service of the poor; and it is in this context that the Holy Father sees fit to make mention of him. The priest in question, of course, is Father Charles de Foucauld.

In November 1963, the bishops of the world who were assembled at Rome for the Vatican Council issued a little known statement entitled, "A Message from the Fathers of the Council to all Priests of the Catholic Church." The message contains the following pertinent passage concerning poverty: ". . . this is most important in our day, that the priest, as Christ, will be the father of the poor and the lover of poverty, and will be able to speak with authority to those innumerable multitudes of less fortunate who are in the greatest danger to their faith."

During the last two decades which preceded the Council, a number of movements have sprung up within the Church dedicated in one form or another to poverty and service. To name but a few, there are the Little Brothers and Sisters of Jesus, the Priests of Prado, the Mission of France, the Worker-Priests, the Disciples of Emmaus of l'Abbé Pierre, the Little Brothers of the Virgin of the Poor, the Jocistes of the late Cardinal Cardijn, and more recently, the Companions of Jesus-Carpenter of Father Gauthier. These movements, too, are certainly harbingers of the new poverty now incumbent upon the people of God.

The strongest argument, however, that poverty is a sign of the times, is found in the conciliar documents themselves. Running as a leitmotif throughout the Decrees, Constitutions, and Declarations of Vatican II are four quotations from the Gospels and Epistles which give the documents significant tone and direction.

First of all, there is the quotation taken from St. Paul's Second Letter to the Corinthians which reads: "Jesus Christ, being rich, became poor for our sakes that, by his poverty, we may become enriched." Next, there is a similar sentence from St. Paul's Letter to the Philippians: "He emptied himself and took on the form of a slave." Then, there is the citation from

St. Mark's Gospel which begins: "I have come not to be served but to serve." Finally there is the quotation from St. Luke's Gospel which goes: "The Spirit of the Lord is upon me. He has anointed me to announce the good news of salvation to the poor." These four quotations revolve about the theme of poverty, humility, and service and, as such, are very significant. Another striking feature of the conciliar texts is the repeated use of the phrases "especially for the poor," and "especially for the afflicted."

The above-mentioned arguments in support of the thesis that poverty is in a special way the will of God for our generation are all taken from within the Church herself. Those from society and the present course of history are equally compelling and forceful.

The overriding problem of our day is the problem of poverty. It is the problem of the rich nations and the poor nations and the ever-widening gap which lies between them. In the last decade or two, this problem has become more and more acute so that today it is like a throbbing migraine headache which not only cannot be ignored but which screams out for immediate attention. Reasons for our growing awareness of this problem are many. Three, however, should be singled out for special mention. These are: (1) the growing interdependence of all peoples on earth; (2) the technological and scientific revolution which has taken place during the last fifty years; and (3) the ascendancy of democratic ideas and ideals throughout the world with concomitant emphasis on the dignity of the individual person.

Ours, in the words of Barbara Ward, is a "spaceship earth." The amazing revolution in the area of communication and transportation which has taken place in the last half-century has destroyed barriers between nations and has narrowed the real distance which separates them. After the coming of jet travel in 1957, no point on earth remains more than twenty-four hours away from any other point on earth. With the development of the supersonic transport in the next ten years this distance will be cut in half again. No major political or social event taking place in the world today requires more than an hour before it is known in the most inaccessible corner of the globe.

What is more, the secret is finally out and the poor of the world today know what their fathers before them did not know; namely, the existence of the undreamed-of luxury and affluence which the other half of the world casually enjoys and effortlessly takes for granted. Moreover, try as they will the affluent ones of the world can no longer keep their heads in the sand and pretend that by ignoring the problem of world poverty it will go away of its own. In all areas of international life—social, political, and economic—men are growing closer together, more aware of one another, and more dependent on each other. This phenomenon has done as much as any one thing to make us aware of the problem of world poverty and has contributed to the sense of urgency which is currently in the air.

A second important factor to be considered is the unprecedented scientific revolution which has erupted in the North Atlantic community nations and has been progressively transforming the face of the earth. Because of man's growing conquest of the forces of nature, men are aware today that poverty is no longer inevitable. The poor can escape from it; they can conquer it; they can control it. Proof that it is possible is the fact that it has been done and is now being done. It has been done in Europe, in America, and it is being done in Russia, Japan, Israel, and Mexico.

The knowledge that poverty is not the inevitable thing that it was always thought to be, but rather a social problem which *can* be eliminated, generates growing malaise in the hearts of the poor. This in turn builds up a moral pressure which is becoming more and more intolerable and which is a source of alarm in all corners of the globe. Fifty years ago, the have-nots of Asia, Africa, and Latin America had a much more fatalistic approach to poverty. Their fathers and their fathers before them were poor. It was always so and it would always remain so. And they bore up under it as best they could without bitterness, without question, and without too much hope.

In recent years all this has changed. The poor today are no longer the lamb-like, submissive, fatalistic creatures they once were. They know that through technological and scientific progress poverty can be changed into prosperity. They are now demanding that chance; they are crying out for a share in the modern revolution, and it will not be easily denied them.

A third factor to be weighed is the spread of democratic ideas and ideals throughout the world. Democracy places unique emphasis on the value of the individual. Democratic society accords uncommon respect to the common man and has given rise to modern concomitant movements of personalism and individual humanism. Progressive democratic leaders have defined the freedoms which the individual should consider his birthright. The United Nations also has declared the basic rights not only of men but of every man. These rights are inborn, innate, God-given. They cannot be violated without violating something which is sacred and divine.

The poor of the world can no longer be spoken of as "hordes" or "masses" or "groups." They are so many individuals with so many individual God-given rights, capacities, and potentialities. This new democratic and utterly Christian view of man has made the problem of man's suffering through poverty, and man's degradation through destitution all the more acute and urgent. All these factors, when taken together, add up to convincing evidence that the twofold virtue of Christian poverty and serving the poor is indeed a "sign of the times," the will of God for our generation, and the wave of the future.

CHAPTER III

The Eternal Poorman

Christ himself was marked by the sign of poverty. He was born under it, lived under it, died under it. If not, we could end this discussion on poverty right here. The fact is, however, the historical Christ chose to be poor and a concomitant fact is, his disciples have no choice but to follow in his footsteps.

The Christian virtue of poverty is based upon faith. Its ultimate justification springs from reasons of the supernatural order. These reasons are a desire to imitate Christ, to live as he lived, and to walk as he walked—in order to be united with him. Suppose, for the sake of argument, that one sold all his goods to give to the poor but there were no poor left in the world to give them to. Suppose, too, that one wished to give alms of all that he possessed but could find no one on the planet who needed or even wanted alms. What then?

If these contrary-to-fact conditions were ever realized, the disciple of Christ would be none the less obliged to embrace a life of voluntary poverty—simply because Christ, his Lord and Master, was poor. This reason overshadows all others and should never be lost sight of.

In the words of Pascal: "I love poverty because Christ loved it." A similar theme is expressed in the prayer of Charles de Foucauld which begins:

"My God I do not see how it is possible for some souls to see you poor and to be willing to remain rich, to see themselves greater than their Master and not wish to resemble you in everything, above all in your abasement. I wish that they would love you, my God, but there is something lacking in their love. I cannot conceive of love without a need, a domineering need to adapt oneself, to make oneself like the beloved. I cannot be rich, at my ease, living comfortably when you have been poor, constrained, living by hard toil."

In the Gospels Christ repeatedly refers to himself as the "Way" and the way is unmistakably associated with poverty and renunciation. *Why* Christ chose poverty is another question: the fact that he did so is clear and, for the Christian at least, there is no escaping its implications.

Sometime ago I submitted a manuscript on voluntary poverty to a priest professor whom I knew for comment and criticism. The paper came back with the withering comment scrawled across the top: "Disquisitions on the nature of Christian poverty are useful only for morons." At first I was bewildered by my critic's reaction, but after reflection I began to understand the reason behind the comment. It was a question of basic outlook. The professor was looking at poverty on a strictly philosophical, intellectual, rational level. On this level it can — and sometimes *does* — come across as something rather meaningless, mindless, even "moronic." On the other hand, I was trying to look at poverty — as did Pascal and Charles de Foucauld — in the light of faith. Here, far from appearing "moronic," it is seen as a spiritual imperative and something which naturally springs from a life of union with Christ.

An important element to bear in mind, also, when considering the poverty of Christ is the element of free choice. St. John places great emphasis on this in his account of Christ's passion and death. No one has the power to take away the life of Christ; he freely gives it. And he gives it in his own good time — not one day or one hour before. From the moment of his arrest until he breathes his last on Calvary, Christ is in complete control of the forces which destroy him. A mere desire on his part would have been enough to bring them to a halt.

This same element of choice, so manifest in the mysteries occurring at the end of Christ's life, is also present in the mysteries occurring at the beginning and middle of Christ's earthly existence. Christ is never the helpless victim of history. His will and his will alone is the moving force which shapes the events and circumstances of his life. Christ then freely and deliberately chose to be poor, to work with his hands, to live the life of an itinerant preacher, and to die the death of a criminal slave. Conceivably it could have been otherwise, but he did not want it to be otherwise.

Thus, by free choice Christ was born under the sign of poverty. At his Nativity angels appeared in the sky and announced the event to the shepherds. The shepherds wondered how they would recognize the new-born infant; and the angels told them: "By this *sign* you shall know him: you shall find the child wrapped in swaddling clothes and lying in a manger." The Son of God takes on flesh and comes to dwell among us. This unspeakable mystery is first announced to the poor in the person of the shepherds, and is stamped for all time by the seal of poverty in the form of swaddling clothes and the manger.

Very often the sharp edges of the sign of poverty under which Christ began his life are blurted by the popular representations of the event which took place two thousand years ago. Countless paintings, drawings, and reproductions have done their work; so that today, when one thinks of the Nativity, one immediately conjures up a scene which is charming, picturesque, and at times, unbearably sentimental. One sees a rosy-cheeked, golden haired child lying on soft yellow straw under a roof of white snow — and overhead, the cool silver stars.

But a stable is a stable, and by any other name will remain the same. There is little of the picturesque or sentimental about a shelter for animals. It is usually dirty, foul-smelling, and unfit for human habitation. It is precisely because a stable lends itself so easily as a symbol of poverty and degradation that the Son of Man chose it for his birth place and as a sign by which men of all time and every place would remember the historical event of his coming.

In passing it should be noted that the interpretation of the manger as a sign of poverty is the traditional one in the Church and an integral part of popular piety. However, in no way does it exclude a "midrashic" interpretation which views the manger not so much as a sign of poverty and lowliness, but rather as a sign that God has now become the food of his people. Just as straw and fodder nourish and sustain animals, so now God becomes the nourishment and sustenance of men. There is no conflict here; simply two complementary ways of looking at one and the same reality — both of which are valid.

That Christ was born in a stable and laid in a manger is startling enough; but after all, this might be passed over as another quirk of history. However, the fact that the event — in sum, *The Event* of all times — is first announced to shepherds makes matters even more astounding.

Not only were the shepherds of Palestine poor and uneducated, but they were legally unclean as well. Their occupation prevented them from fulfilling the manifold prescriptions of the law as interpreted by the Pharisees. Thus, they became ritually contaminated and, in a sense, social pariahs and outcasts. Christ began his life in despicable poverty and went first and foremost to the despised poor and lowly.

Later on Christ became known as a carpenter and the son of a carpenter. He came from a little known hamlet in a small conquered country of the Middle East. He chose to be known not as "Jesus of Jerusalem" or "Jesus of Rome," but as "Jesus of Nazareth." He lived the life of a poor itinerant preacher who had nowhere to lay his head and who depended on the charity of others for his sustenance. He had no money to pay the temple tax; and, at times, his disciples picked grain from the fields because they had nothing to eat. He had no formal education, no diplomas; and, during his entire life-time, he never traveled more than three hundred miles from the place where he was born. His closest companions were a group of poor, uneducated fishermen.

The prophets of the Old Testament, especially Isaiah and Zechariah, foretold a Messiah who would be poor and lowly. This has been the tradition of the Church for more than two thousand years; and the evidence from the Gospels and Epistles supporting this thesis seems overwhelming. Still there are many who are unwilling to accept the fact that Christ really was of the poor and by personal experience knew the meaning of poverty and deprivation.

While their arguments are many, one of the favorites seems to be the fact that Christ was a carpenter. A carpenter, they reason, is an artisan; and an artisan in the Palestine of Christ's day belonged not to the class of the poor, but rather to the comfortable, well-off middle-class. Conclusion: comfortable, middle-class aspirations are perfectly reconcilable with a desire to imitate the historical Jesus of Nazareth.

Most of those who question the poverty of Christ *do* concede at least that during his public life Christ conveyed the general impression of being poor. However, if Christ chose to live thirty years of his life in relative, artisan-type, middle-class comfort, and only the final three years, or one-tenth, of his life in poverty, then his personal invitation to poverty pales somewhat, and the desire to imitate him in one's own life tends to fade.

However it is at best doubtful if the craft of carpenter in a poor hamlet such as Nazareth was very lucrative. It is also uncertain whether those who practiced this trade were appreciably, if at all, better off than the general mass of the poor.

For example, Joseph of Nazareth, the foster father of Jesus, was an industrious and hard working carpenter — at least one can reasonably presume so. But he did not grow rich from his trade. The fact that he remained a member of the lower-class is brought out in the episode of the presentation in the Temple. Joseph and

Mary, being devout Jews, scrupulously kept all the prescriptions of the Law, including the yearly pilgrimage to the Holy City. However, forty days after the birth of Jesus, when they brought the child to Jerusalem to present him to the Lord, they could not afford to offer a lamb in sacrifice. In a pastoral country, such as Palestine, a small lamb could not have been prohibitively expensive unless one was very poor. Joseph and Mary, instead of purchasing the more expensive animal, bought two turtle doves which the Bible describes as "the offering of the poor."

Furthermore, just as today, so too, one may assume, in the time of Jesus, there are carpenters and carpenters, not all of whom fare the same. For example, the standard of living of a carpenter in Korea today is somewhat higher than that of a farmer, a day-laborer, or a factory worker. An historian writing two thousand years from now about an individual Korean carpenter would automatically assume that he was better off than the masses of the people. This does not always follow.

For example, I myself am acquainted with three carpenters who were members of my former parish here in Pusan. Carpenter Kim is somewhat better off than his neighbors and can be described as a member of the upper lower-class. Carpenter Choi and Chang, however, share the same, grinding poverty as the majority of people in this area. Carpenter Choi has tuberculosis and can work only sporadically; for him at least, the trade of carpenter is not at all synonymous with material security and well-being. Carpenter Chang, however, is able-bodied. He works from dawn to dusk, and he works well; but he is a "hoin" (a "good guy") and this happy character trait is his economic undoing. Often he works for gratis for those too poor to pay; and when he does earn a little money, importunate friends and relatives, usually poorer than himself, are close at hand to see to it that he does not keep it for long. On the face of it, then, it would seem too facile to conclude that Jesus was of the middle class simply because he practiced the trade of carpentry.

Jesus chose the trade of carpenter not for reasons of material benefit or social security, but rather because of its intrinsic value as a *sign*. Considered as a sign of one who works with his hands and earns his bread by the sweat of his brow, the choice of carpenter serves perfectly. It is a sign which cuts through social strata, transcends boundaries of space and time, and is easily grasped and understood. Everyone who lives in a house with doors, windows, beams, and furniture, has some idea of what it means to be a carpenter. For example, if Jesus chose to be a farmer or a fisherman, those unfamiliar with the soil or the sea would have difficulty grasping the meaning of the sign. There is no such difficulty with one who works with wood and uses axe, hammer, plane and nails. These tools are among the oldest in the world and they have changed remarkably little throughout the centuries.

In a sense, the trade of carpenter is unique and Jesus chose it primarily because of its value as a sign of poverty, humility, and lowliness. He chose it for the same reason he chose the sign of the swaddling clothes and the manger at his birth, and the sign of the cross at his death.

The "internal" evidence that Christ was of the poor is equally persuasive. This evidence comes across forcefully in Christ's words and actions. Christ not only went to the poor but, what is equally astounding, he preached to them a gospel of poverty. He said: "Blessed are you poor; blessed are you who suffer; blessed are you who weep; and blessed are you who hunger." The poor, the hungry, and the suffering who heard these words did not laugh as perhaps they would have if Christ had belonged to the rich, ivory-tower upper-class. Nor did they reject him as a hypocrite or as an idealist with his head in the clouds. Christ's words rang true as a bell, and he spoke them with authority — the authority of the Son of Man who knew by experience the meaning of poverty and destitution.

I imagine Christ in Korea today where the socio-economic conditions are so remarkably similar to those of the Palestine of his day. It is a cold, windy day in February and Christ is walking along the seashore here in Pusan. He comes upon a group of women-divers gathered on the rocks. They are huddled together warming themselves about a small, blue-smoke, flickering fire made of drift wood. The faces of the women — browned, cracked, leathery — tell of an existence almost unbelievably cruel. But they are tough — the toughest of the tough — and they have almost forgotten what it means to complain.

Christ approaches them and repeats to them the words he addressed to his disciples in the sermon on the plain: "Blessed are you who are poor, for yours is the kingdom of heaven."

It is April now and Christ is walking in the fields near here. He comes upon a group of three people trying to break the hard brown earth with a plow. Too poor to afford an ox, a man and a woman are strapped to the plough and an old man is guiding it. Backs straining, forehead veins standing out, and faces flushed, they relax and stand still as the mysterious stranger approaches them. He says: "Blessed are you who hunger now for you shall be satisfied. Blessed are you who weep now for you shall laugh."

Christ is in the city now talking to the "wisaengwon." These are members of the "honey bucket brigade" — those who earn their living emptying toilets and carrying the night soil away in heavy wooden buckets hanging from yokes across their shoulders. Christ says to them: "Blessed are you when men despise you and reject you. Rejoice and be glad for your reward in heaven shall be great." The "wisaengwon," as did the poor who heard Christ speak the same words 2,000 years ago, would say: "He does not speak to us as one of our leaders or politicians, but he speaks as one having authority."

There may be those who question the fact that Christ lived under the sign of poverty; but none question the fact that he died under it. He freely chose the death of the lowest slave and the poorest criminal. Sold as chattel for 30 pieces of silver and stripped of all possessions, he gave all that he had to give. And as a final sign, his crucified, broken, naked body was laid to rest in a borrowed tomb.

Such is the Christ of history and the Christ of the Gospels. He is a poorman — and he is "the same: yesterday, today, and forever."

CHAPTER IV

God's Elite

Christ not only lived poor and died poor, but he went to the poor as well. According to the mind of Christ, the poor have been chosen by God to enjoy his special favor. They have first right to the good news of salvation and a privileged position in the kingdom of heaven.

From the very outset, Christ made it clear that the Church which he had come to establish was to be primarily a "poor man's club." Unlike most clubs, however, which are organized along social, economic, or professional lines Christ's community was to be completely free from snobbery, exclusivism, or discrimination. His would be a Church of the poor, but a Church of the poor open to everyone — including the rich and the middle class.

At the time of Christ, the people of Israel could be divided roughly into four groups: (1) the Pharisees — religious leaders of the Jews, scrupulous observers of the law, lovers of money, and hypocrites; (2) the Sadducees — aristocrats, landowners, and collaborators with the Roman occupiers; (3) the Essenes — ascetic, austere-living, pre-christian monks; and (4) the people of the land — the great mass of the disinherited, the have-nots, and the never-had's. Christ chose to associate himself in a special way with the last of these four groups and the Sadducees and Pharisees found this hard to understand.

There are many elements which group men together and separate them from one another. Among these are race and nationality. These "vertical" elements, so to speak, are physical and easily recognizable. There are other characteristics, however, which separate and divide just as radically as do race and nationality. For example, poverty and destitution.

Poverty, misery, and destitution have as much impact on the psychology of a given people as do race, culture, and nationality. Hunger has a language which only the hungry can understand. In many respects, a Jew who is hungry has more in common with a Greek or a Roman who is in similar need than he has, for example, with another Jew who is a stranger to the world of want and suffering. "Vertically" people are united by race. "Horizontally" they are united by a common economic and social bond.

God thrust himself into the history of man on two occasions, each time to make a choice. The first choice was on a "vertical" level. Yahweh selected the sons of Abraham, Isaac, and Jacob and established a convenant with them. He would be their God; they would be his people. Their descendants would be as numerous as the stars of the heavens and the sands on the seashore; and they would have a destiny above that of all other nations.

God's choice of the Jewish people was determined by race and blood. Within this given people, however, God was preparing another more radical choice which was to be made by his Son and which was to transcend racial and blood lines. This second choice, established on a "horizontal" level, centered on the people of the land. In these last days, then, before the second and final coming of Christ, it is no longer the Jews nor the poor Jews, but the poor *period* who have become the chosen people, the new Israel, and the elite of God.

Christ's predilection for the poor is described in all the Gospels but in a special way in the Gospel of St. Luke, the so-called "social evangelist." According to St. Luke's Gospel, the first public pronouncement of the Savior is a proclamation of his messianic mission to the poor.

During a visit to his home town of Nazareth Christ entered the synagogue for the Sabbath service. The Book of Isaiah was brought to him to read. He opened it and began the reading with this passage: "The spirit of the Lord is upon me, wherefore he has anointed me to preach the gospel to the poor." As the first public pronouncement of the Messiah these words are tremendously significant and they indicate clearly the direction Christ's ministry among men was to take.

Looking at the same passage from Isaiah in a slightly different light one still arrives at the same conclusion. In the Palestine of two thousand years ago, all that most men had to offer in return for wages was the labor of their bodies. If their bodies were broken or deformed, they had little, if any, labor to offer; and naturally they received little, if any, wages in return. The lepers, the lame, the blind, and the deaf — whom Christ mentions — were not only physically handicapped, they were usually materially destitute as well. More often than not they were forced to beg for a living. One thinks of the cripple begging at the temple gate whom St. Peter healed or again the beggar born blind whom Christ cured in the temple on the Sabbath-day. What is more, society treated these as guilty of sin, accursed by God, and as so many burdens to be shunned. Christ comes primarily to heal and to help such as these. In this passage, then, Christ proclaims his mission and that of his Church as a twofold one of service and salvation — primarily of the poor.

Again following the Gospel of St. Luke, Christ's first major address, his sermon on the plain, begins with the words: "Blessed are you poor, for yours is the kingdom of God." It is important to note that the term "poor," when used by St. Luke, means just that; namely, those who are really and effectively poor — not those who are poor in spirit of whom St. Matthew writes. As for the term "Kingdom of God," it is used in the Gospel in a dual sense. It refers both to God's celestial kingdom, heaven, and also to his terrestrial kingdom, the Church. With this in mind, one can properly paraphrase St. Luke's first beatitude to read: "Blessed are you poor, for yours is the Church."

This same relentless theme of the Church-of-the-poor-open-to-everyone-even-the-rich is expressed in equally forceful language in the Epistle of St. James. In the second chapter of this Epistle, St. James writes: "Harken, my dearest brothers, has not God chosen the poor in this world rich in faith and heirs to the kingdom which God has promised to those that love him." The kingdom of heaven, but also the kingdom of God upon earth, namely, the Church.

The theme of God's choice of the poor occurs again in the fourteenth chapter of St. Luke; this time in parable form. The story concerns a certain rich man (God) who prepared a great feast (eucharistic banquet) and invited many guests. When everything was in readiness, the servant of the rich man went out to summon those who had been invited only to discover that because of material concerns, they all had made other plans. One had bought a farm, another a yoke of oxen, one had married a wife. All hoped that the master of the house would understand and hold them excused. Unfortunately, the master did not understand and he did not hold them excused. Instead, he became angry and he said to his servant: "Go out quickly into the streets and lanes of the city and bring in here the poor and the weak. . . ." In God's scheme of things, the poor and the weak are destined to enjoy the privileged position forfeited by the rich and the powerful.

God's choice of the poor is also the theme of the *Magnificat*. In this song of joy and hope Mary draws on the purest current of spirituality of the Old Testament and projects it into the New. "And Mary said: 'My soul proclaims the greatness of the Lord because he has looked upon his lowly handmaid. . . . He has pulled down princes from their thrones and exalted the lowly. The hungry he has filled with good things; the rich he has sent away empty.' "

Mary indirectly acknowledged God's preference for the poor when she herself appeared to the children of men to entrust them with a message or a mission. At Guadalupe, for example, she appeared to a poor, uneducated Aztec Indian. At Lourdes she chose

Bernadette whose family was sheltered at the time in an abandoned city jail. At Fatima she selected Lucy, Francisco, and Jacinta — all children of poor peasant parents. In 1933 at Banneux, Belgium, Mary appeared to a poor 12 year old child by name of Maria Beco and said: "I am the Virgin of the poor." Other examples which come to mind in which the visionaries were all from the common people are La Salette, France, and Beauraing, Belgium.

St. Paul eloquently expresses the same theme in his First Letter to the Corinthians when he writes: "Take yourselves, for instance, brothers. At the time when you were called; how many of you were wise in the ordinary sense of the word; how many were influential people, or came from noble families? No, it was to shame the wise that God chose what is foolish by human reckoning, and to shame what is strong that he chose what is weak by human reckoning; those whom the world thinks common and contemptible are the ones God has chosen — those who are nothing at all to show up those who are everything."

Not only did the Son of God show his predilection for the poor by words, but by his life and actions as well. Throughout his public life, Christ was never far from the common people. He immersed himself in the crowds which at times were so thick that people trampled each other and at other times even prevented him from eating his meals. He remained close to them; so close that they touched him with their hands and felt the healing power flowing from his body into theirs. Sinful women were permitted to wash his feet with their tears, and dirty, runny-nosed little children were allowed to climb upon him to receive his blessing.

In the seventh chapter of St. John's Gospel, one of the Pharisees unwittingly revealed what type of person Christ was when he said: "Not one of the notables or Pharisees has believed in him, but only this rabble who do not know the law and are accursed." As a matter of fact, it has been said that Christianity is the only movement in antiquity which began with the masses of the poor and which developed and spread not among the notables, the wealthy, or the so-called elite, but among the "rabble."

St. Peter and St. Paul are excellent proto-types of this Church-of-the-poor-open-to-everyone-even-the-rich which Christ established. In the Acts of the Apostles, St. Peter proclaimed: "Gold and silver I have not . . ."; and in his Epistle to Timothy, St. Paul, the Apostle who worked with his hands, wrote: "Money is the root of all evil. . . ."

If Christ came primarily for the poor, what is to be said of the rich? Did he simply write them off? Not at all. He loved them with the same infinite love as the poor; but, at the same time, he condemned their attachment to material wealth.

It is not easy to separate evil from the evil-doer; yet, Christ always did so. In imitation of Christ, the late Pope John also practiced this beautiful distinction of charity. Pope John embraced all men, including communists, atheists, and materialists as his brothers. He showed them the same warm, simple, outgoing love. At the same time, however, he condemned the evil with which they were associated; and he never watered down the doctrine of Christ in order to make it more palatable to them.

Although Christ always identified himself with the poor, he did nothing to shun the rich and the powerful. On occasion, he dined with them. And he invited them time and time again to enter his kingdom, the Church; but always on his terms, not theirs. Some accepted; most did not. Among those who accepted Christ's invitation on his terms was Matthew, the former tax-collector. After meeting Christ, Matthew gave away his wealth to the poor and followed him. Another example is that of Zacchaeus who, after meeting Christ, gave half his wealth to the poor and promised to make restitution to anyone whom he had previously defrauded.

Some of Christ's most severe maledictions fell on the heads of the rich. These must have been filled with wonder at Christ's words because at that time wealth was considered a sign of God's favor and poverty a sign of his disfavor. It is true that the prophets had taught differently, but their message went unheard.

In all the pages of the New Testament, the two things which Christ condemns the most are hypocrisy and material wealth — in that order. Christ's speech was always yes-yes, no-no, never maybe. So it is that when he finished speaking about the evil of material riches, there was no doubt as to where he stood. For example, when Christ spoke of money, he would say: "What men hold up in esteem, God holds in abomination." And again: "No man can serve two masters; you cannot serve God and money." When speaking of the wealthy, Christ would say: "Woe to you rich. . . ."; or again: "Sell what you possess and give it away in alms."

The Church of the New Testament is clearly seen, then, as the Church-of-the-poor-open-to-everyone-including-the-rich-and-the-middle-class. It has taken the Church just twenty centuries to come full circle so that today we have a Church of the middle class and the wealthy which is — more or less — accessible to the poor.

According to the Lucan Gospel, Christ's credentials as Messiah were challenged for the first time by the disciples of the imprisoned John the Baptist who sought him out and bluntly asked: "Are you the one who is to come? Or should we look for another?" Christ told them to return to the one who had sent them and report what they had seen, to wit: "the dumb speak, the deaf hear, the blind see, the lame walk, the lepers are cleansed, the dead rise, and the poor have the gospel preached to them."

The disciples of John knew that Isaiah had foretold that the Messiah would heal the sick, raise the dead, and preach the gospel to the poor. Christ was doing just that and he points to this fact as proof of his authenticity. Such were his credentials and the disciples of John went away convinced.

If the disciples of the Baptist were to return to earth today, they would ask for the Church the same series of questions they asked of Christ. "Are you the one who is to come? Or should we look for another? Are you the City of God, the New Jerusalem, the Expected of the Nations? Or should we go elsewhere?"

In reply, the Church would say: "See for yourself, the poor of the world have the Gospel preached to them."

And the disciples of John would have to answer: "*Do* they?"

Statistically, the evidence is to the contrary. The poor of the world — at least 85% of them — are in Africa, Asia, and Latin America; while 85% of those commissioned by God to announce the Gospel to them — priests, brothers, and sisters — are elsewhere. They are mostly in America and Europe where the land is fat and the people who dwell therein rich. Can it really be said, then, that there is a massive, concerted, selective effort on the part of the Church today to seek out the poor of the world and to bring them the message of salvation?

Let's consider it another way. According to the Kenedy Directory there are approximately 248,000 priests, brothers, and sisters in the United States. Of this number only about 11,000 are serving on the missions. And of this latter number, only half are serving the poor on the missions; the other half are serving the rich or the middle class. This leaves us then with the dismaying figure of 2% of our American Church personnel directly engaged in the service or apostolate of the poor in the third world of hunger.

Of course many more American priests, brothers, and sisters are ministering to the poor within the United States itself. It's hard to get an accurate figure, but let's be generous and say that they number 7%. This still leaves us with a total figure of only about 9% of American Church personnel announcing the Gospel to the poor of the world — hardly enough to convince the disciples of John the Baptist that the poor today *do* have the Gospel preached to them.

Furthermore, since an army, albeit a spiritual one, marches on its stomach, can it be said also that there is a mounted program on the part of the Church to fully support its world-wide mission to the poverty-stricken? Once again the evidence is to the contrary. To give but one typical example: in a year when the Society for the Propagation of the Faith in the United States collects only $13,000,000 for support of the Church's world-wide mission program, dioceses such as New York and Brooklyn collect $35,000,000 and $45,000,000 respectively for their own local building programs. The rich churches get richer and the poor churches continue to get the crumbs.

Oversimplified? Perhaps. Yet nothing is quite so simple and straightforward as the words of Christ when taken at face value. No hemming or hawing; no qualifying or modifying; no if, but, or maybe. Just: "the poor of the world have the Gospel preached to them," period.

CHAPTER V

Why Christ Chose Poverty

In foregoing chapters, we saw how Christ's life was marked not only by the sign of poverty, but by the sign of service and apostolate to the poor as well. The question to be examined here is, "Why?" Why did Christ choose to be remembered by the sign of the stable and the carpenter's tools rather than by the sign of intellectual achievement, political power, or material wealth? Why also did Christ choose to identify himself with the poor and lowly rather than with the rich or middle class?

The answer to these questions is found in St. Paul's Epistle to the Hebrews. In chapter 2 of this Epistle we read this verse: "Therefore he had been made like his brothers in every respect so that he may become a merciful and faithful high priest in the service of God to make expiation for the sins of the people. Because he himself suffered and was tried, he was able to help those who are tried." Christ came to serve as mediator between God and man. He is the eternal high priest, the *pontifex*, the bridge-builder between heaven and earth. Since the overwhelming majority of the human race, at the time of Christ, today, and during the period in between, are and were of the poor, it is but natural that Christ should identify himself with this class in order to fulfill his role as mediator of humanity.

It is estimated that the population of the world today is 3.5 billion people — a figure which is equal to, if not greater than, the total number of men who were born on this planet before us and who have since passed away. The cumulative historical population of the world is estimated to be 7 billion. Of this number it is estimated that 6 billion people were and are of the poor. Less than 1 billion were and are of the affluent middle-class or beyond-affluent upper-class.

Someone sent from above to serve as the representative of men would naturally associate himself with the 6 billion under-privileged majority rather than the relatively small 1 billion privileged minority. It seems logical that once Christ decided to become man, he would decide at the same time to become a *poor* man as well.

Christ, the poor man, stands before God to make a new promise in the name of humanity and to seal it in his blood. Through this new convenant, Christ promises in our name to love, serve, and obey God; God in turn promises to provide for our needs, watch over us, and protect us. We will be his children; he will be our Father.

Through the Old Testament, God became the Father of Israel and the Jews became his chosen people. The old agreement was made by Moses in the name of the Jewish people and ratified in the blood of bulls. It now passes away and makes room for the new.

Christ made the new promise *primarily* in the name of the 6 billion under-privileged majority with whom he associated himself in a special way. However, as we have already pointed out, there is no room in the New Testament for the type of spiritual snobishness which the children of the Old Testament were prone to practice. The New Testament, made primarily — but not exclusively — in the name of the poor, leaves ample room for the 1 billion rich minority. They too can participate in the fruits of the new promise on conditions spelled out by Christ in the pages of the Gospel. Christ admits that these conditions are quite stringent; but with God's help they are not impossible, "for all things are possible with God."

The second part of the previously cited verse from the Epistle to the Hebrews emphasizes the fact that Christ himself "suffered and was tried" in order that he might "help those who are tried." Christ knows the meaning of pain, poverty, and deprivation not theoretically or speculatively but by personal experience. He drank to the dregs the cup of human suffering of every man. No man, no matter how deep his pain or how crushing his humiliation, can look up at Christ and say, "You do not know what it is." He *does* know what it is because he has experienced it himself.

It is in this sense that St. Thomas Aquinas explains the meaning of the enigmatic phrase of the Apostles' Creed: "On the third day, he descended into hell." St. Thomas maintains that this means that Christ, in some unknown, and as yet unexplained way, tapped the depths of all human pain, suffering, and humiliation.

Christ personally descended into the hell of extreme poverty in order that those in similar conditions may look to him for the strength and courage to go on. The psychiatrist who can address his patients with the words: "We neurotics"; or the priest who can say to his penitents: "We sinners"; or a Father Damien who can begin a sermon with the words: "We lepers," have much more power to heal and to help than those who know only in a theoretical manner the pain of those to whom they minister. In much the same way Christ can turn to the have-nots of the world and say, "We poor," and the poor know that it is so.

While examining reasons for Christ's choice of poverty, mention should be made also of its salvific aspect. Very often we take too narrow a view of the mystery of redemption. We tend to condense it into the limited series of events which occurred at the end of Christ's 33 years on earth, namely, his passion, death, and resurrection. Granted that these mysteries are by far the most important; still they are not exclusive.

Christ redeemed us, not only by his passion, death, and resurrection, but by his entire life on earth as well. Christ's whole human existence, from the moment of his conception to the time of his ascension, takes on a redemptive quality and a salvific aspect. St. Paul brings this out quite clearly in his Letter to the Corinthians when he writes: "Christ, being rich, became poor for our sake that by his poverty we may be enriched." In the light of this text, it can be stated that Christ by freely taking upon himself a life of poverty, obtained grace and merit for us. Just as through his death Christ obtains life and, through his suffering, joy; so also through his poverty he obtains spiritual riches for the people of God.

St. Paul, in writing to Timothy, suggests that because we are co-redeemers with Christ, we must make up in our own bodies the sufferings which are lacking in the body of Christ. In a similar manner, it can be said that we must also make up in our own lives the poverty lacking in the life of Christ — in order to participate more fully in the redemption of the poor.

Just as there exists a law of nature which governs the play of the stars and the movement of the seas so too there exists a supernatural law of salvation which remains constant and which runs throughout the mysteries of Christ's life and death. This law is expressed in many ways in the pages of the New Testament, but most succinctly perhaps in St. Paul's Letter to the Corinthians when he writes: "But the foolish things of the world has God chosen to put to shame the wise; and the weak things of the world has God chosen to put to shame the strong, and the base things of the world and the despised has God chosen, and the things that are not. . . ."

In the eyes of men, nothing is more foolish, weak, base, despised, and "not," than suffering and poverty. Yet the law of salvation dictated that through these very things God's power and glory were to be manifested. Adhering to the dynamics of this mysterious law, Christ achieved his glorification through the freely-accepted humiliation of a life of poverty and a death preceded by intense suffering and pain.

This amazing theme of Christ's glorification-through-humiliation is eloquently expressed in the Gospel of St. John. In this Gospel Christ repeatedly referred to his approaching suffering and death in terms of exaltation and fulfillment. For example, Christ said: "The hour for the glorification of the Son of man is at hand." And: "If I be lifted up from the earth I will draw all things to myself."

As has been previously mentioned, the mystery of the crib and the cross are in essence one and the same. The supreme humiliation — and concomitant glorification — achieved at Calvary was already begun at Bethlehem and experienced in a lesser degree during the years separating these two great mysteries. Rejection, suffering, and death are extreme forms of humiliation to which Christ submitted himself at the end of his life in order to complete what went before and in order to achieve ultimate glorification.

Once the law of glorification-through-humiliation is acknowledged, it is difficult to imagine how the drama of Calvary could have been preceded by anything other than a life of poverty on the part of Christ. The degree of poverty and the form of poverty may be open to dispute, but the *fact* of the poverty of Christ was pre-determined by this divine law of salvation.

A life of poverty is a humiliation less extreme than suffering and death, perhaps, but nonetheless real and authentic. In the eyes of the world, there is nothing exalted about being born in a stable or fleeing to a foreign country to live there the life of a displaced person. Furthermore, daily manual labor such as Christ performed causes fatigue and pain, which in turn has a humbling effect on the flesh and spirit of man. Christ further humiliated himself by accepting the insecurity and "foolishness" inherent in the life of an itinerant preacher who came from Nazareth and who had no fixed abode.

After his resurrection Jesus appeared to the disciples on the road to Emmaus and said; "Ought not the Christ have suffered these things in order to enter into his glory?" The "things" which Christ endured in order to achieve fulfillment and glorification include the birth in a stable and the life of freely-accepted poverty as well as the suffering and the death.

In the closing paragraphs of this chapter let us examine another reason for God's predilection for the poor — this one based upon the revelation that God is love. In the Old Testament God's love for the people of Israel is compared among other things to the love which binds a mother to her children. A devoted mother loves all her children with equal affection, but shows special tenderness for the one child among them who happens to be the weakest, the most needy, and the most suffering.

Just as such a child has special claim on its mother's heart so, too, do the poor of the world have special claim on the heart of God. The rich, armed as they are with the power of wealth, are better able to fend for themselves and in a sense do not have the right to make the same demands upon God as do the poor. For example, the money of the rich man provides him with many things including the necessary leisure to think about God and the eternal truths. It also permits him to travel to places of pilgrimage, to study at great universities, and to buy books to read about God if he is so inclined. Moreover, as honey attracts bees, so, too, does the wealth and power of the rich man attract religious teachers, chaplains, priests, and sisters in abundance. They will care for his soul with great devotion in the name of building up an elite for the Church of God. At the same time they will not be above gathering in the crumbs of prestige and power which from time to time fall into their laps from the rich man's overloaded table. Such is not the case with the poor. And this is one reason why God does not hesitate to give them priority and privilege among the people of God.

In the Gospels, Christ said: "Blessed are you poor for yours is the kindom of Heaven." And again: "Unless you first be converted and become as little children, you cannot enter the kingdom of heaven." In a spiritual sense, the poor resemble

little children and this is why Christ used the two terms inter-
changeably.

A small child is unable to satisfy his most basic needs. He
is completely dependent upon his parents and must surrender
himself to them in order to survive. Christ tells us that the ideal
attitude of man toward God resembles the attitude of a little
child toward his parents. Finite and sinful man must realize that
of himself and by himself he is utterly helpless to satisfy his
most basic spiritual needs. He is absolutely dependent upon
God for all that he has and all that he is in both the natural
and supernatural order.

Just as a child depends upon his parents, so, too, does the
poor man depend on others to satisfy his most basic needs.
The poor man is neither self-sufficient, independent, nor secure.
He is at the mercy of forces above and outside of himself and
over which he has little or no control. Just as a small child must
look to his parents, so, too, the poor man must look to divine
providence to provide him with food for his body and nourishment for his soul.

The only attitude which becomes man — poor, sinful, struggling creature that he is — when he stands before God is the
attitude of the child towards his parents and the poor man
toward the world. This attitude is essentially one of utter help-
lessness, complete dependence, and absolute surrender. Of its
very nature, it is an attitude more easily come by on the part
of the poor than on the part of the rich. Poverty which is humbly
accepted brings with it an inner experience of one's weakness
and leaves one spiritually cleansed.

God resists the proud and gives his grace to the humble.
This could hardly be otherwise because pride is essentially a
lie and God loves people too much to encourage them in a way
which is false. This is why Christ spoke so often of poor men
and children, why he said: "I have come not for the well but
for the sick ... not for the just but for sinners ... not for those

who see but for the blind." This, too, is one reason why Christ himself chose to identify himself with the poor and to live a life of personal poverty. In the light of the Gospels and Epistles, this choice seems to be an altogether natural expression of the same divine love which brought Christ to earth in the first place.

Facing the Poor

This may be a bit unusual in that it consists almost exclusively of photographs. It is intended as a visual aid — or background music, if you like — to accompany the reflections on service of the poor which are to be found in this book.

In reading a work of this nature it is so easy almost unconsciously to fall into the error of thinking that poverty is mostly statistics, facts, and figures. Poverty is more than this; it is above all **people.**

Poverty has a human face and a human heart. True, its face is not always pretty to look at. And at times its heart, too, is badly scarred, even twisted. But until we get into the habit of looking poverty squarely in the face and seeing there the image of the Poorman of Nazareth we are approaching the problem in something less than a Christian manner.

The photographs which follow should be viewed as imperfect portraits of the poverty of Korea, India, Africa, South America, Appalachia and Harlem — impoverished symbols of the poor of the world — including those of the States.

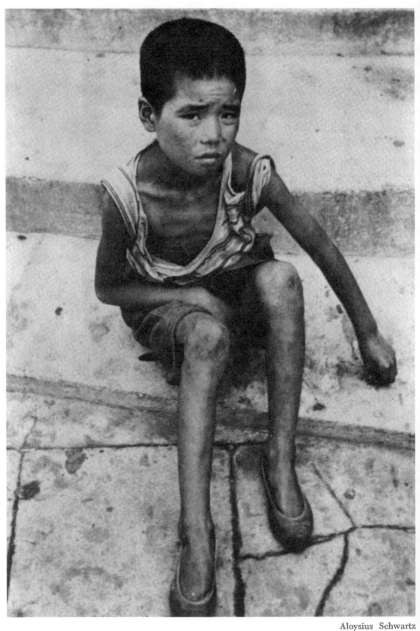

Aloysius Schwartz

"And thy own heart a sword shall pierce, that the thoughts of many may
be revealed." (St. Luke)

Richard Finke

Aloysius Schwartz

"Today no one can be ignorant any longer of the fact that in whole continents men and women are ravished by hunger, countless numbers of children are undernourished, so that many of them die in infancy, while the physical growth and mental development of many others are retarded."
(On The Development Of Peoples)

"Whatever is opposed to life itself such as subhuman living conditions . . . as well as disgraceful working conditions . . . are infamies indeed . . . they are a supreme dishonor to the Creator." (*The Church In The Modern World*, 27)

"We'll sing in the sunshine and we'll laugh everyday . . ."

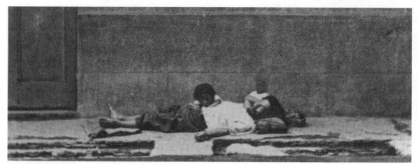

"Feed the man dying of hunger, because if you have not fed him, you have killed him." (St. Ambrose)

"I'm goin lay down my burden, down by the riverside, I ain't goin study war no more."

Aloysius Schwartz

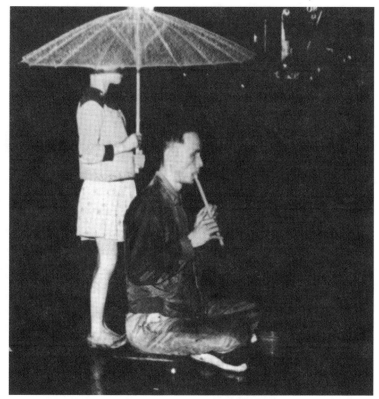

"Jesus answered: 'He was born blind so that the works of God might be displayed in him.'" (St. John 9, 3)

Richard Finke

"Lord, when did we see you hungry?" (*St. Matthew*)

"*Therefore there must be made available to all men everything necessary for leading a life truly human, such as food, clothing and shelter; the right to choose a state of life freely, and to found a family, the right to education, to employment, to a good reputation, to respect...*" (*The Church In The Modern World*, 26)

Aloysius Schwartz

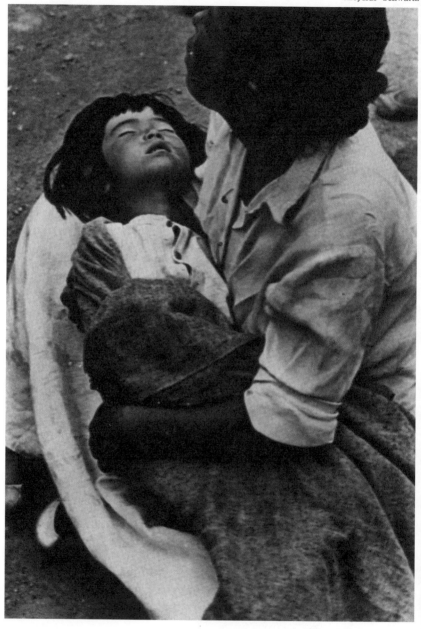

"Lord, when did we see you sick and did not minister to you?"
(St. Matthew)

"The people who walked in darkness have seen a great light: upon those who dwelt in the land of gloom a light has shone." (*Isaias* 9, 1)

Alba House

"The future's not ours to see, whatever will be will be . . ."

Aloysius Schwartz

"Blessed are the breasts that nursed thee..." (St. Matthew)

CHAPTER VI

Church of Poverty

The Church is the "sacrament of Christ" and "the projection of Christ in time and space." To be faithful to her mission the Church must mirror her Founder in all things. As Christ, then, the Church too must be marked by the double sign of poverty and service of the poor.

The exact nature of the community which Christ came to earth to establish was first revealed in the episode of the three temptations in the desert. Occurring as they did just before Christ began his ministry among men, they are most significant and merit reflexion in depth.

In the first temptation, the devil said to Christ: "Command this stone to become bread." And Jesus answered: "Man shall not live by bread alone." By rejecting this temptation, Christ rejected the notion of a materialist Church, a Church of eating and drinking, of wealth and riches. His Church was to be primarily one of poverty.

"Then the devil took him to the holy city and set him on the pinnacle of the temple and said: 'If you are the Son of God, throw yourself down for it is written "he will give his angels charge of you and on their hands they will bear you up lest you strike your foot against a stone."' And Jesus said: 'You shall not tempt the Lord your God.'" What would have happened if Jesus had consented to do as the devil suggested? If Jesus had cast himself down unhurt from the temple, the crowds of people which were always milling about below would have been dazzled by this spectacular display of power over nature and they would have rushed to believe in Christ. Their faith would have rested not on humility but on Christ's visible triumph over the laws of creation. By rejecting this second temptation, Christ rejected a Church of triumphalism, a Church which seeks to sway men by power, glory, and prestige. His Church was to be a Church of humility.

In the last temptation, the devil took Jesus to a high mountain and showed him the kingdoms of the world and the glory thereof and said: "All these I will give you if you kneel down and adore." And Jesus said: "Be gone, Satan!" By rejecting this temptation, Christ rejected the idea of a brick and mortar Church, a Church whose strength can be measured by the number of its buildings or the amount of money in its banks. His Church was to be a spiritual kingdom of poverty and humility whose strength and vitality can be measured only by the charity which burns in the hearts of its members.

All three synoptic writers recorded the episode of Christ's temptations, and the question comes to mind: How did they know about it? Other than the three principals themselves, Christ, Satan, and the Angels, there were no witnesses. Yet, both Matthew and Luke describe the event in detail and Mark at least makes mention of it. One is led to assume that Christ himself related the episode to the apostles because of its great importance in shedding light on the nature of the Church which he had come to establish. And that nature, as we have seen, is neither power, wealth, nor prestige; but rather poverty, humility, and service.

Another episode in the life of Christ which gives us insight into the nature of his Church concerns the money-changers in the temple. According to the Gospel of St. John, this episode too occurs near the very beginning of Christ's public ministry.

It is the feast of the passover and the vestibules of the temple are filled with merchants and money-changers. The sounds of the clinking of coins and the haggling over prices float into the temple and mingle with the prayers of the pilgrims. Upon viewing the scene, Christ is filled with anger, and the Lamb of God suddenly becomes the Lion of Judah. He makes a whip of cords and the arm made strong by twenty years of manual labor wields it with authority. The merchants cringe and duck and try to save themselves as best they can from the fury of this seeming madman.

At first glance, it does seem that Christ's reaction to the money-changers is somewhat out of proportion to the reality. After all, many of the temple pilgrims came from Syria, Egypt, and other foreign lands and money had to be changed into the local currency. And after changing money, oxen, sheep, and doves had to be purchased for the sacrifice. What is so wrong about all this?

It were as if Christ were to enter St. Peter's Basilica in Rome today and bodily eject the merchants who sell there the tickets to ride the elevator to the Dome. Or as if Christ, at St. Mark's in Venice, were to turn over the stalls of those who collect the "offerings" of the tourists as they enter.

In the episode of cleansing the temple, as in so much of what occurs in Christ's life, the action is both real and symbolic. It fits a given historical situation and, at the same time, it looks to the future. Christ, realizing the terrible damage that money could and would do to his Church, casts it out of his temple as he would a devil out of one possessed. The Gospel narrative relating the event ends on a note of almost poetic poignancy. While the leaders of the Jews are left raging and fuming, the voices of children are heard singing in the temple *"Hosannah to the Son of David."* The message seems to be this: a Church of poverty, while alienating the proud and the powerful, will attract the child-like and the innocent. It is in this spirit that Christ in another place in the Gospels voiced the prayer: "I give you thanks, O Father, because you have hid these things from the wise and prudent and reveal them to little ones."

In the miracle of the multiplication of the loaves and fishes, Christ provided us with still another lesson concerning the nature of his Church. After miraculously multiplying the loaves and the fishes Christ instructed his disciples to distribute them to the people. After eating, the people realized what a good thing a full belly is and they rushed to make Christ king. Christ fled from them because he wanted faith freely given, not coerced by offering free food to poor people.

St. Paul went even further. He did not want to persuade people to believe even by the power and eloquence of his words. In Corinthians 2:3-5 we read: "And I was with you in weakness and in fear and in much trembling, and my speech and my preaching were not in the persuasive words of wisdom but in the demonstration of the spirit and of power that your faith might rest not on the wisdom of men but on the power of God." No pressure or persuasion here, only profound respect for the freedom of the individual conscience.

Here the question arises: If we are so scrupulous about the means employed, how will we ever fill our churches with new converts? The majority of converts in pagan lands come in search of truth, yes; but in varying degree also in search of free food, medicine, housing, and a host of other material benefits as well. Is all this to be thrown out the window? The answer, as gleaned from the pages of the New Testament, seems to be a qualified "yes." Let us examine this important question in more detail.

According to the teaching of St. Paul, faith ideally should be made to rest on the power of God and not on the wisdom of men. Moreover, Christ, especially in the Gospel of St. John, hinted at a mysterious pre-destination which has already taken place in the hearts of men. For example, he said: "Those whose works are good will come to a knowledge of the truth"; and again, "Those who are of God will hear the word of God." *Theoretically,* it would seem to be enough to present the Gospel message in all its purity and simplicity, then sit back and let the Spirit do the rest.

This purist view, however, must be carefully modified in order to reflect faithfully the mind of Christ. Christ's view of man as seen in the New Testament was always a very balanced one. He never addressed himself to man as to a philosopher or an angel, but always to the flesh and blood creature that man is. Christ took into consideration the fact that the average man is more swayed by what he can touch and see than by what he hears; that he is led to accept a given truth more because of emotional reasons than because of spiritual or intellectual ones; and that in the final analysis, he believes more with his heart than with his mind.

Take for example the miracle of the loaves and fishes. In order to lead the people to a spiritual truth, Christ placed into their hands the everyday, comforting substance of bread. The people felt it, tasted it, ate it. Through this sensory, physical reality Christ intended to lead the people to accept the eternal truth that he is the life of the world. Unfortunately, the people got no further than the material reality, and because their faith rested *entirely* on this, Christ rejected it.

Another example of this principle is seen when the disciples of John came to interrogate Christ. Christ told them to return to John and report not only what they had heard but what they had *seen* as well.

When Christ sent his apostles and disciples out into the villages of Palestine he instructed them to do two things, first, preach the kingdom of God, and second, *heal the sick*. Christ, then, intended service to go hand in hand with an apostolate to the poor. However, this service should be viewed primarily as witness and sign. It is a palpable witness to God's love and a visible sign of the coming of the "kingdom of concern" among men.

St. Paul himself followed these general guidelines. As Christ, his Master, he too on occasion raised the dead, healed the sick, and cast out demons — primarily as a sign pointing to the presence of "the kingdom." The modern equivalent of the miracles of Christ are social service and the corporal works of mercy. These are less dramatic and startling than the miraculous events recorded in the New Testament perhaps, but they can achieve the same effect. They can speak the language of love just as well and lead men just as effectively to embrace the kingdom of God.

If Christ had not performed his miracles of service the only ones who would have believed in him would have been some philosophers perhaps, a few saints, and the angels in heaven. His message would have been lost on the average flesh and blood man in the street for whom it was primarily intended.

The faith of the average convert in mission lands rests on motives which are always a generous mixture of the spiritual, emotional, and physical. To insist on a faith which is 100% pure is to insist on something which only the angels in heaven are capable of giving — and which Christ himself did not seem to demand in his day. As long as a convert's motives for believing are not *preponderantly* material, he should be welcomed into the Christian community and the community should then undertake the never-ending task of perfecting the neophyte's faith.

The purist or fundamentalist would do well to ask himself the question: What were the apostles' motives for believing in Christ in the first place? The answer is, they were convinced that Christ's kingdom was primarily a political one and they wanted a share in it. Their original motives, then, seem to have been an amalgam of political ambition, earthly desire, and spiritual aspiration. It wasn't until Pentecost that they really began to understand what it was all about. Christ, however, saw that they were basically men of good will, so he realistically accepted them as they were — and went on from there.

Christ's public ministry was characterized by four features: personal poverty, living as and with the people, service of the poor, and apostolate to the poor. In the missionary discourse, pronounced first to the twelve apostles and later on to the seventy-two disciples, Christ instructed his fledgling Church to adhere to the same general guidelines. First, poverty: "Take nothing, no money nor gold or silver . . . not even a few coppers for your purses." Second, live as and with the people: "In whatever house you enter, stay there and eat what is given you; don't go from one place to another." Third, service: "Heal the sick, cure the lepers, raise the dead, cast out devils." And four, apostolate: "And he sent them to proclaim the kingdom of God . . . and they went from village to village proclaiming the good news."

It is nice to dream of a Church according to the Gospels — a Church of poverty, humility, and service. It is even more consoling to dream that the masses of the poor, with joyful and illumined expressions, will march in procession to enter such a Church. Unfortunately, the second part of the dream is pure illusion.

Christ did say that his Church was to be characterized by poverty, humility, and service but nowhere did he say that these qualities were guarantors of success. On the contrary, he ended his missionary discourse with the sobering warning: "They will hand you over to sanhedrins and scourge you. You will be dragged before governors and kings. You will be hated by all men on account of my name." Such was the treatment that Christ, the poor servant of Yahweh, received; such, too, would be the treatment that a poor servant-Church could expect.

Christ, despite his many signs and sermons, had a hard time indeed in getting his followers to accept the notion of a Church of poverty. They found the idea of a political, triumphalist Church more appealing and they clung to it to the bitter end. At the Ascension, for example, the apostles stood there looking up after Christ had disappeared into the clouds of heaven. What were they looking for? They were half expecting, half hoping, that Christ would return immediately in glory to set up his earthly and political kingdom. Two angels sent from above broke in upon their reverie with the question: "Why do you remain here looking up?" It required ten days of intensive prayer and the coming of the Holy Spirit before the apostles' vision of a triumphalist Church gave way to that of a Church which is poor and servant.

From its very inception, the Church was plagued by the "mammon of iniquity." The first procurator in the history of the Church, Judas Iscariot, turned out to be a thief and a traitor also. Hardly had the Church been born when two of its members lied to the Holy Spirit because of money, and the punishment meted out to Ananias and Sapphira was nothing less than death. Again, when the early Church was subject to its first temptation to simony by Simon the Magician, St. Peter thundered: "May your silver perish with you because you thought you could obtain the gift of God with money."

Not only at her inception but throughout her history, the Church has been harrassed by the same temptations which confronted Christ in the desert, especially the temptation to money and wealth. As early as the third century, in the writings of the Shepherd of Hermas, the Church was compared to an old woman seated in an easy chair, well-fed, well-heeled, and well-satisfied. In the thirteenth century, St. Francis of Assisi was instructed by Christ to re-build his crumbling Church and the principal tool used in this reconstruction was poverty. Again in the sixteenth century, the bishops and cardinals assembled at Trent declared that the greatest evil affecting the Church at that time was the evil of material riches. More recently, the Council Fathers of Vatican II emphasized again and again the present-day danger of wealth, materialism, and triumphalism to the Bride of Christ.

One day, so the story goes, St. Dominic was being shown around the city of Rome by the reigning sovereign pontiff. After conducting the saint through the city, and pointing out all its pomp, splendor, and riches, the pope turned to his guest and said: "The Church can no longer say, as did St. Peter in the Acts of the Apostles, gold and silver I have not." St. Dominic, replying as only a saint could, said: "By the same token, the Church can no longer say, 'take up thy crutch and walk.' "

A Church of the poor, marked by poverty, humility, and service, is a Church of miracles. A Church of the rich and middle-class, marked by wealth and triumphalism, is a Church which has lost its élan and is as salt which has lost its savor.

CHAPTER VII

The Virtue of Christian Poverty

The virtue of poverty may be considered in two ways; one, in relation to Christ the eternal poorman, and two, in relation to the poor whom we shall always have with us. Here we shall treat only of the first and leave the latter for consideration in a subsequent chapter.

The virtue of poverty springs primarily from a desire to imitate Christ and to model one's life after that of his Lord and Master. It is deeply rooted in faith and charity, and as such it is above all a person-to-person relationship with the living Christ.

This "personalist" approach to poverty cannot be over-emphasized. Moreover, it is not accurate to think that this is merely a question of semantics. It is much more than this – it is a question of fundamental outlook.

Christianity is above all a person-to-person relationship with the living God. It is significant that nowhere in the Gospel does Christ say: "My *doctrine* will give you life," or "My *teaching* will show you the way," or "Truth is to be found in the *revelation* which I leave you. . . ." Rather, Christ unequivocally states: "*I* am the way, the truth, and the life"; "*I* am the light of the world . . ."; and "*I* am the resurrection."

As a Christian, then, I do not believe so much in some*thing* as in some*one*. I do not believe in a set of dogmas or concepts or in a lifeless "ism"; but I believe first and foremost in the God of Abraham, Isaac, and Jacob, and in his only begotten Son, the real, living, historical Christ.

In much the same manner, I do not believe so much in the poverty of Christ as in the poor Christ. And primarily because of this inner encounter with Christ the poorman, I, too, desire to be poor. In one of his Epistles St. Paul wrote the following autobiographical sentence: "It is no longer I who live, but Christ who lives in me." Christ in a very sense *re-lived* in Paul — and, in a lesser degree, *re-lives* in every Christian after him — the eternal mysteries of his poverty, passion, death, and resurrection.

A personalist view of poverty will help to keep it in perspective and balance. It will prevent one from making a fetish out of poverty or from building around it one's own little personal monomanias. To imitate Christ, then, means to imitate the *whole* Christ, who is not only a poor man but also the humble servant of Yahweh and the completely self-giving "man-for-others" as well. A style of poverty which is proud, brittle, or self-conscious in no way resembles that of Christ.

Much is being said and written today about the evils of economic poverty. In fact, a type of moral warfare is being waged on all fronts to eliminate it from the face of the earth. Today, as never before, there is great emphasis on human progress, self-development, and personal fulfillment. In this context many people find it difficult to accept poverty as an ideal valid in itself and as a condition necessary for a full Christian life.

The saints, however, encountered no such difficulty. Their lives were characterized by a movement — gradual or sudden — away from wealth, comfort, and possession toward poverty, simplicity, and renunciation. This inner élan on their part arose not so much from a desire to identify with the poor of the world or to serve humanity, from a desire to be united with God and to serve him alone. In other words it is more theocentric than anthropocentric; more Christocentric than human-centric.

St. John the Baptist, the last of the prophets and the pre-cursor of the Christian saints, is a good example of this. Why, it may be asked, did John live in the desert, eat honey and locusts, and wear camel skin? Was it in order to serve his fellow man or to contribute his share of human progress? Judging from the Gospels, such does not seem to be the case. Rather his choice of a life of poverty was based on a spiritual intuition which in-dicated that this was the path which lead to union with God.

St. Paul is another example. As Christ his Master, he too, by deliberate choice, worked with his hands and exposed himself each day to the pain, humiliation, and insecurity of material poverty. "Each day I die," he wrote in one of his Epistles. This strange inner élan on the part of the saints, so contrary to that of the world and the flesh, has its source in the Holy Spirit — the same Spirit who led Christ into the desert for 40 days where there was only sand, calcified rock, locusts, wild honey, and solitude.

Later on we see the same irresistible force at work in the heart of a St. Francis of Assisi. St. Francis passionately sought out what he himself referred to as "*Donna Poverta*" basically for one reason — in order to achieve deeper union with Christ. So, too, was the case with St. John of the Cross. He set for himself the ideal of "*nada*," nothingness, namely for one reason: in order to ascend more easily Mount Carmel where union with God awaited him. St. Benedict Joseph Labre and St. Peter Alcantara are two more examples which come to mind of saints who pushed the ideal of poverty to the limits of human en-durance as a natural expression of their will to imitate Christ and their desire to be united with God.

Of course one cannot imitate the poor Christ without, at the same time, being consumed with a desire to give himself to others, to serve society, and to help humanity. All the saints previously mentioned who adopted poverty as an ideal valid in itself were, at the same time, completely altero-centric. They did effectively, and at times heroically, serve the poor whenever the occasion presented itself.

The question which comes to mind at this point is: How should one attempt to imitate Christ in his poverty?

In attempting to answer this question, some people become strangely slavish, literal, and fundamentalist in their outlook. For example, Christ worked with his hands; so, too must they. Christ had a low-protein, low-calorie diet; so, must they also. Christ begged for a living, lived in the fields, and had only one or two changes of clothing; so, too must they.

Such a rigid, unbending view of poverty is not in the spirit of the Gospels. The poverty of Christ seems to have a flexible, easy, "stay-loose" quality about it. Christ himself personally adopted the poverty of his day. His life of poverty was lived simply and naturally in a frame of reference based on the socio-economic condition of the Palestine of 2,000 years ago. He did not intend to set a detailed pattern which was to be slavishly followed by every man no matter what place, time, or social condition in which he is born.

In speaking of this free-flowing nature of the poverty of Christ, however, one must be careful not to water it down. One should always bear in mind that the poverty of Christ was real, everyday, poor man poverty. In other words it hurts. There are no two ways about it, "poor man" poverty — such as Christ lived — is painful. It causes discomfort and demands sacrifice to endure. At times it is noisy, robs one of privacy, and smells. At other times, it humiliates, irritates, and makes one insecure. Such poverty requires great selflessness to sustain voluntarily over a long period of time.

Father Antoine Chevrier, founder of the Priests of Prado, once remarked: "Where there is not some suffering, there is not true poverty. True poverty is a form of suffering." In a similar vein, St. Francis de Sales wrote: "To wish to be poor without suffering any inconvenience is to wish the *honor* of poverty and the convenience of wealth."

It is difficult to lay down a hard and fast set of rules to govern the practice of Christian poverty. This is for each to decide in the forum of his own conscience. However, a few general guidelines may be helpful.

First of all it is important for one imbued with an ideal of voluntary poverty to know himself and to work carefully within his own physical and psychological limitations. In trying to conform his life to that of Christ the poorman, one may never overstep these built-in natural boundaries. An attempt to do so would be presumptuous.

However, one should take a dynamic, rather than static, view of his limitations. With effort, they can be stretched and what may not be permissible one year is quite possible the next. For example, let's say that psychologically you have "need" of a radio because of the tension-release which it provides. Maybe next year, however, with a little effort, you will find that you can do without a radio and still not expose yourself to undue tension. Or, maybe a few years ago, you found that living in a small room and sleeping on the floor was too constraining and just a little beyond your strength. Now, however, you are perfectly at ease in these circumstances. In other words, one's acceptance of his natural physical and psychological limitations is not closed and definitive but open and generous.

In passing, it should be pointed out that one's *real* physical needs are rather few and relatively easy to satisfy. These consist mostly of the food, shelter, and clothing necessary to sustain and protect life. One's psychological needs, however, are something else. They are extremely complex and today they are being multiplied at a dizzying pace. Although physically one needs very little, psychologically one "needs" a spacious home with all its modern, mechanical wonders; one "needs" a car, a stereo, a color TV set, a three week vacation in the summer, a trip to Europe, a yacht, and so on. These needs are artificial, and sustained at fever pitch by the advertising media of our consumer-economy. Partially as a result of this, most people in

American society seem to be suffering from what has been aptly described as "an overloading of the sensory media."

The Christian ideal is a constant reduction of one's psychological needs until there is a gradual melding of these and one's real physical needs. This ideal perhaps is attainable only by a Francis of Assisi or a John of the Cross. Nevertheless there should be a constant inner tension and striving towards it.

This "inner tension" or "striving towards" can be best expressed by the single phrase "will-to-be-poor." This expression, more than any other perhaps, sums up the basic Christian attitude towards the virtue of material poverty. Implied in it is a constant dissatisfaction with the status quo and a concomitant movement towards a life of greater simplicity and renunciation.

The will-to-be-poor should not be confused with mere wishful thinking. For example, one consents to the ideal of poverty in the abstract and even says to himself: "Yes, poverty is a good thing and someday I intend to do something about it. But not now, Lord. Later." This is what is meant by wishful thinking. Cardinal Newman referred to this as "notional" assent which is quite different from "real" assent. The will-to-be-poor, in order to be real and authentic, must express itself by constant effort towards the Gospel ideal and must be accompanied by sacrifice, struggle, and self-inflicted discomfort.

If one possesses the will-to-be-poor and is sincerely trying to implement it while working carefully within his own physical and psychological limitations, the situation — at least from a Christian point of view — is basically a healthy one. Whether the person in question be rich, poor, or in between, is secondary. As long as this basic Gospel tension really exists and it is not just something imaginary, it can be said with assurance that one is following "the Way."

In this chapter it may be well also to develop more fully a paradox which has already been touched upon lightly. The paradox I refer to is the seeming contradiction between a desire to imitate the poor Christ of the Gospels and a concomitant desire to lift the poor of the world out of their misery.

This in a sense is a classical, biblical paradox. In the opening pages of the Bible we read the injunction that man is to increase and multiply; he is to fill the earth and subdue it. Man is to go forward and onward. He is to dominate the forces of creation and put them at the service of humanity. This is a clear call to progress. At the same time, the New Testament in equally clear terms issues an invitation to imitate Christ in his life of poverty. How are these apparently conflicting tensions to be reconciled?

The secret lies in double spiritual vision; that is, a Christian's view of reality should at the same time be both eschatological and incarnational. When looking at himself the Christian's outlook is eschatological. He is longing for the second coming of Christ and his constant prayer is the cry: "Come, Lord Jesus, come!" During this short period of time before the *parousia* the disciple of Christ possesses things as not possessing them. He tries to slough off all the frills and non-essentials of living in order to be free to serve his Lord and Master. Since here on earth the Christian is a pilgrim with no lasting city he travels light and is constantly on his guard against accumulating unnecessary possessions.

Looking away from self towards his neighbor, the Christian's viewpoint shifts. His outlook is no longer eschatological, but primarily incarnational. Considering his neighbor, the follower of Christ acts as if the only thing that counts is the *here* and *now*. Consequently he does everything possible to alleviate his neighbor's suffering and everything within his power to heal and to help the poor of the world. However, the Christian's attitude should never become so incarnational that he frees the poor man from his bonds of economic servitude only to deliver him over to the equally degrading slavery of avarice and materialism. It is necessary, then, to strike a proper balance between the inner-

directed eschatological outlook and the outer-directed incarnational viewpoint. If one possesses a real will-to-be-poor and a
will-to-serve according to the mind of Christ one will quickly
realize that the difficulty here is more imagined than real, and
the contradiction is found more in fancy than in fact.

Before ending this chapter some mention should be made
also of what is at times loosely referred to as "Christian humanism." Implied in this is a philosophy of "the good life" which at
first glance seems at odds with an ideal of Christian poverty.
The hero and undeclared patron saint of the so-called "Christian
humanist" is St. Thomas More. This poor martyred saint is usually pictured in the imagination of his adepts as comfortably
seated in front of a roaring fire, reading the latest writings of
Erasmus with a glass of brandy nearby. The little known fact is,
however, that St. Thomas More lived a life of great austerity,
wore a hairshirt, and was more familiar with Sacred Scripture
than the secular writings of his day.

The goal of all personal humanism including the Christian
variety is self-fulfillment. The means to this end as outlined in
the Gospels is not through acquisition, but renunciation; not
through riches, but poverty — and this remains one of the supreme paradoxes of Christianity. It is in this sense that St. John
of the Cross wrote: "If you wish to possess all things, renounce
all things: if you wish to be all in all seek to be nothing in
nothing."

If anyone directly seeks to fulfill himself, the goal will inevitably elude him. Self-fulfillment is the natural unsought-after
by-product of a life of self-forgetfulness. Christ said: "He who
seeks his life will lose it . . . and he who loses his life will find it."
In so doing one becomes a real person and, in a sense, an integral
Christian humanist. There is a great challenge here; but unfortunately only the saints have had the courage to put it to a
test.

All this of course is anathema to the secular humanist. Yet
it is difficult to imagine more real and completely fulfilled human

beings than, for example, a Francis of Assisi, Christ's singing troubadour, or a John of the Cross, one of the greatest lyric poets in the history of Spanish literature. In their scale of values — and that of the Gospel — simplicity and poverty, far from being a hindrance are a help to someone imbued with an ideal of true Christian humanism.

CHAPTER VIII

Poverty of Spirit vs. Material Poverty

Oh Poverty of Spirit, what crimes are committed in thy name! The revelation of Christ concerning the evil of material riches is forthright and explicit and there is little room for misunderstanding. Yet one frequently finds the strong wine of this doctrine diluted with vague and watery references to poverty of spirit. The resulting mixture, tasteless and insipid, goes down as effortlessly as a long drink of water.

It is perplexing how people will read, retain, and repeat what St. Matthew has to say about poverty and yet never give St. Luke so much as a glance. The two writers, however, complement each other and, when taken to-gether, present the revelation of Christ on the subject in its full scope.

St. Matthew writes: "Blessed are the poor in spirit." He means blessed are those who are inwardly detached from all created things including their own will and who, at the same time, joyfully accept their complete dependence on God.

On the other hand, St. Luke writes: "Blessed are you poor." Not poor in spirit, but *poor,* and he means just that. According to St. Luke, those who live lives of everyday, down-to-earth, material poverty have a right to consider themselves blessed and happy. Their happiness is based on hope — hope in a new heaven and a new earth in which the present order of things will pass away and be replaced by something as yet undreamed of.

From the above it becomes clear that poverty of spirit and material poverty cannot be dissociated. They go together like body and soul. This is the hard doctrine of Christ and few there are today who seem willing to accept it. This is hardly surprising for even at the time of Christ, the apostles found this particular doctrine "stupefying." This is brought out in the episode of the rich young man as recorded in the Gospel of St. Mark.

A rich young man came to Christ and said: "Good Master, what must I do to gain eternal life?" Christ replied that he should begin by keeping the commandments. The rich young man answered that he did keep the commandments; in fact, he had been keeping them even from his youth. In that case then, Christ said: "Sell what you have and give to the poor and come follow me."

The young man was thunderstruck. He loved God and kept the commandments and, who knows? maybe he even had poverty of spirit. At the same time, however, he had much wealth and Christ's suggestion that he give it away was considerably more than he had bargained for.

As the rich young man walked away, Christ turned to the disciples who had witnessed the scene and said: "How difficult it will be for those who have wealth to enter the kingdom of heaven. It is easier for a camel to pass through the eye of a needle than for a rich man to enter the kingdom." St. Mark concludes the episode with the single comment: "At these words the apostles were stupefied."

Man is a creature composed of two elements: body and soul, matter and spirit. To treat man as a disembodied spirit, or as a soulless body, would be absurd. It is equally unrealistic to accept Christ's teaching on poverty of spirit without at the same time accepting his teaching concerning material poverty. It smacks of hypocrisy to speak of poverty of spirit while one is living in the lap of luxury and is surrounded by material comfort and ease. On the other hand, it is equally false to speak of material poverty when one has nothing but, at the same time, is eating his heart out with avarice for material wealth.

There is a striking parallel between the doctrine on faith and works as set down in the writings of St. Paul and St. James respectively, and the doctrine on material and spiritual poverty as recorded in the Gospels of St. Matthew and St. Luke. In his Epistle to the Romans, St. Paul seems to say that man is justified by faith alone. St. James clarifies this by stating that faith without works is meaningless. In a similar way, St. Matthew speaks of poverty of spirit while St. Luke in his Gospel shows how it is incomplete unless accompanied by material poverty.

Faith, like poverty of spirit, is an intellectual attitude, a spiritual adhesion, an inner conviction. Of itself and by itself it is not enough. In the second chapter of his Epistle, St. James writes: "And if a brother or sister be naked and want daily food and one of you say to them 'go in peace, be warmed and filled,' yet you do not give them these things that are necessary for the body what shall it profit; so faith, also, if it has no works is dead in itself." Again in the same letter, St. James writes: "Faith without works is sterile." The same may be said of a poverty of spirit divorced from material poverty: it too is dead and sterile.

Christianity is the religion of the Incarnation. As such, it always deals with man, not as an abstraction, but as the concrete flesh and blood reality which he is. Nothing is more realistic nor has a surer ring of inner truth than the Gospels and Epistles. It is marvelous to read, for example, a St. Paul stating as he does in Romans, "I believe," and St. James following this up immediately by saying, "Prove it!" In a similar manner, St. Matthew says, "I am poor," and St. Luke immediately counters by saying, "Show me!"

Someone who pretends to be poor in spirit, yet gives no evidence of it in reality, may be compared to someone who is very fond of drink yet insists it has no hold on him. Those who know the person suspect that he is already in the first stages of alcoholism. Yet the person maintains that he is free, detached, and independent from it. "I can take it or leave it," he says, and he says it so often that he finally convinces even himself that it is so. At all times, however, there is a bottle on this person's shelf; and as iron filings to a magnet, he is drawn to it at various times of the day and night. If the person were truly free and independent from drink, if he really could leave it, then there should be some evidence of this in his daily life. He should be able to prove it by giving up alcohol completely, by doing without it for a long period of time, or by reducing the intake to a negligible quantity. Otherwise, he leaves himself open to the charge of hypocrisy.

Money, comfort, and possessions can exert as strong a hold on an individual as drink on an alcoholic. A person pretends to be free, detached, and independent from these things. He insists he is poor in spirit, he is indifferent to them, he can take them or leave them. Yet, it is a moral drama for this person to give a really generous donation to the poor. If the person's wealth is threatened, he panics; and if the comfort to which he is attached is removed for even a short period of time, he becomes excessively irritable and unhappy. The first step in the rehabilitation of an alcoholic is to get him to admit that he *is* an alcoholic, and then to go on from there. It is similar with someone attached to money, possessions, and comfort. If he recognizes the fact, and is willing to admit that he has the disease, then there is hope. If not, dry rot has already set in and there is not too much one can do to remedy the situation.

In one of his Epistles, St. Paul wrote: "I know how to live in abundance and know how to live in want." In this one sentence, St. Paul captured once and for all the essence of Christian poverty in all its freshness and spontaneity. From this, it can be seen that poverty is not so much a question of how much or little one possesses, but rather how detached and free one is from his possessions. There is a saying in French which, when translated, goes something like this: "A monk may have only a nail in his cell, but he still can become attached to it."

It is necessary to add immediately, however, that detachment from material things runs the risk of being mere wishful thinking unless it has been tested in the fire and water of real, everyday, physical poverty. It is difficult to approach the heart and center of Christian poverty and discover its hidden promise of spiritual freedom while one is living in the lap of luxury. It can be done, perhaps, but it is something extremely difficult to achieve in this flesh and blood world of ours.

CHAPTER IX

Poverty as Sign and Witness

Just before his death Christ made the statement: "I have come into the world to bear witness to the truth." Jesus bore witness to the truth throughout his life both by his words and by his actions. Everything he did and *was* served as sign; it said something to men.

Implied, then, in Jesus' life of poverty and indentification with the poor is the important element of sign, witness, and attestation to a truth other than itself. What truth, precisely, does the poverty of Christ bear witness to? What is it a sign of? What does it say to men?

It says, in language far more dramatic than words, that ours is no lasting city, that we are pilgrims of the eternal, and that we should possess things in this world as possessing them not.

Christ's poverty turns the attention of men away from such things as what they shall wear and what they shall eat and directs it towards the ultimate goal of all human existence which is the kingdom of God and his justice. It is a luminous sign pointing to a transcendent truth other than itself.

Christ's witness to poverty also contains a certain element of shock. Christ's manner of acting and living profoundly disturbed people, it shook them up, and it made them ask searching questions. For example, in the Gospels we see the leaders of the Jews asking themselves the question, "What manner of man is this who goes about stirring up the people?"

Judging from his Epistles, St. Paul gives the impression that the apostles too were in the habit of upseting people both by what they said and were. St. Paul describes them as "A spectacle to angels and to men," and as, "Fools for Christ's sake." To be an effective "spectacle" one can not hide his light under a bushel; rather he must hold it up high for all to see.

So it is that Christ himself not only was poor but what is equally important he *appeared* poor as well. Christ's poverty was not only interior, but exterior as well. As a matter of fact, his whole life and manner of doing project a clearly visible image of renunciation, humility, and service of others. From this we can deduce that a given sign in order to be effective must be seen; and witness in order to be relevant must be exteriorized.

Christ did nothing to conceal the fact of his birth in a stable. On the contrary, it was announced from the skies by an army of angels. Nor did Christ in any way try to hide the fact that he worked with his hands — something which in his day was looked down upon. This too was public knowledge, and people, upon looking at him, would ask, "Is this not Jesus the carpenter?" Christ's material poverty, during his itinerant life, was equally open and visible. He called attention to it when he said, "The foxes have dens and birds of the air have nests; but the Son of man has nowhere to lay his head."

We can conclude then that it is not enough for a disciple of Christ merely to *be* poor. What is equally important he must *appear* poor as well. It is not enough to live a life of poverty; it must also be exteriorized. In order to be completely faithful to the poor Christ of the Gospels, one's life must be a sign and a witness; it must shake people up and in a sense be a "spectacle." All this is possible of course only if one is willing to let his light shine before men.

The Vatican II *Decree on the Appropriate Renewal of the Religious Life* has this to say on the subject: "Poverty voluntarily embraced in imitation of Christ provides a witness which is highly esteemed, especially today. Let religious painstakingly cultivate such poverty, and give it new expressions if need be. By it a man shares in the poverty of Christ, who became poor for our sake. . . . Religious poverty requires more than limiting the use of possessions to the consent of superiors; members of a community ought to be poor in both fact and spirit. . . ."

Many clerics and religious today live lives of genuine austerity and simplicity. Unfortunately, however, they effectively conceal the fact behind a facade of wealth and power. They protest that they are poor as church mice, and very often they are. Still, they do not *appear* so to the man in the street; and, in this measure at least, their poverty no longer resembles that of Christ. Very often a misguided pre-occupation with prestige and/or economy effectively robs a life of real poverty of its value as sign and witness.

For example, I myself am acquainted with a saintly prelate whom I shall refer to as "Bishop Christopher." Although Bishop Christopher privately lives like a pauper, he gives the impression to the man in the street of living like a prince. His own personal life is characterized by great simplicity. For example, he sleeps on a board, always sits on a hard straight-back chair, never eats meat, fish, or eggs and is given to various other laudatory ascetical practices. On the other hand, however, his public life projects an image of wealth and ostentation. Although bishop of a city which boasts some of the worst slums in the world, he lives in a spacious, richman's dwelling surrounded by trees, shrubs, a flower garden, a gold fish pond, and many of the other good things of life. Pressing close up against the protective walls of his residence are the huts and hovels of the poor. One can not help but wonder what these think of a summer evening as they look down from their teeming, stinking, rat-infested hovels to see His Excellency strolling among the cool trees of his garden reciting his breviary.

In Bishop Christopher's defense, however, it must be said, that he is convinced that his style of living is contributing to the honor of God and the glory of his Church. He reasons that if he were to adopt a more modest mode of living, the rich, the elite, and the intellectuals — all those who in his frame of reference really count for something — would look down upon him and the Church. In the name of prestige, then, a life which could very easily bear witness to the poverty and humility of Christ becomes, in the eyes of the poor, a stumbling block and, in the bad sense of the word, a "sign of contradiction."

As Bishop Christopher, so too the Cardinal of Sao Paulo, Brazil, lives in a palace — a *crumbling* palace left him by his predecessors, but a palace nonetheless. It too is surrounded by a lovely park and a flower garden. The Cardinal, however, has opened wide the gates of his residence and invited his neighbors in. They have accepted the invitation with delight; and it is a joy to see today neighborhood children running and playing on the Cardinal's grass as if it were ordinary grass, and the neighborhood mother resting nearby in the shade of the Cardinal's trees as if they were ordinary trees. What could be more simple, natural, and spontaneous than this? Yet, often that's all it takes to remove the egotistical element out of clerical wealth and transform it into a humble sign of service.

Not only pre-occupation with prestige, but concern with economy as well often prevents a life of poverty from serving as a sign and witness. A good example of this is brought out in the life of Father Vincent Lebbe.

Father Lebbe, a famous Belgian missioner to China who died in 1940, possessed a mystique of Christian poverty similar to that of Francis of Assisi and Charles de Foucauld. Among many other undertakings, Father Lebbe founded a community of Chinese sisters based on the twofold ideal of poverty and service. Father Lebbe's idea of poverty, moreover, was not something he got out of a spiritual manual but rather it was inspired by the lives of the dirt-poor Chinese peasants who dwelled in that region. In other words, it was "poorman" poverty.

One day, a new convent was being built and the Sister in charge of construction came to Father Lebbe with a problem.

The problem was whether to put rice-paper or glass windows in the new convent. True, rice-paper was cheaper and was used by all the poor of the region; but, Sister argued, glass would be more economical in the long run since it did not have to be frequently repaired and replaced as was the case with rice-paper. Father Lebbe listened to Sister's defense of glass and then quietly shattered it with the single remark: "Sister, remember: you have taken a vow of poverty — not economy."

I myself have seen another good example of this classic conflict between economy and poverty enacted here on the local Korean scene. A group of Korean Sisters, dedicated to poverty and service of the poor, known as the "Mariahwe," thought it but natural that they wear the inexpensive "komusin" (rubber shoes) as do most poor women in Korea. The other Korean sisters who wear the more expensive leather shoes felt threatened by this innovation and they quite naturally objected. They pointed out with familiar logic that since their leather shoes did not have to be frequently replaced as was the case with the "komusin" they were more economical in the long run and thus more in keeping with the vow of poverty. All of which may not be false, but the Mariahwe Sister in charge answered: "When we appear before God on judgment day, Christ is not going to ask how much money we have saved or how economically we have lived, but rather how *poor* we have lived."

It must be admitted, however, that at times this tension between economy and poverty is not so easily resolved. Especially does the problem become acute when a new building has to be constructed for community needs. With all the good-will in the world, it is not possible to build an *old* convent. What is more, by the mere fact that a convent is new and big, it tends to appear rich, imposing, and, in a sense, a counter-sign to poverty and humility.

With a real will-to-be-poor, however, and a little imagination the problem can be circumvented. An example is the recently completed Motherhouse of the Mariahwe Sisters mentioned previously. The crumbling barracks which originally housed the group had become too small for the rapidly-expanding community. The decision to build could be delayed no longer but the agonizing question arose: How to build a new convent which was not only simple and poor but also *appeared* such? At the same time, the building should not be artificial, uneconomical, or impractical. Finally, after much thought, a two-story center building was erected. The lower floor contains the refectory which also doubles as a lecture hall and recreation room. The second floor houses the chapel. The building, although strong and adequate, is quite simple and completely devoid of bell-towers, verandas, and other architectural gingerbread. Around the center house seven, small, Korean-style cottages have been built. Each cottage contains four rooms, each of which can accommodate three girls. These rooms are used for sleeping and studying.

This approach to the problem of building a new convent was actually a little cheaper than putting all facilities under one roof but this is not the point. The point is, apart from the psychologically-enriching family atmosphere provided by cottage-style living, the convent itself appears poorer and more simple than one main building could.

The convent serves as a sign and a witness to poverty and humility not only to outsiders but, more important, to candidates entering the community as well. To a great extent, one's surroundings condition one's thinking. As Frank Lloyd Wright once put it: "First you form the building, then the building forms you." In the same line of reasoning, it is difficult to think poor while one is living rich and while one is psychologically identified with a convent which appears prestigious and imposing. The fact that the Mariahwe candidates live in a building of utmost simplicity facilitates a deeper penetration of the Christian ideal of poverty and service.

Since the Mariahwe Centerhouse is located on a large piece of property, part of the land was used for family-unit orphanages.

The orphanages could have easily been built elsewhere; but by deliberate choice they were constructed close to the center building. Apart from other considerations, the orphanages, too, serve as a sign: they tell onlookers that the community — its possessions and its personnel — are dedicated to service of the poor and needy.

In discussing poverty as witness, the question inevitably comes up: Is it possible for an *American* to be a sign of the poverty of Christ in Asia, Africa, and Latin America? There is such a monumental gap between the standard of living to which the American has been accustomed and that of the people among whom he lives that at first glance the problem would seem to be insurmountable.

For example, the average per capita income in Korea is about $120 *per annum* as compared to $3,500 in the U.S.A. A difference of almost 30 to 1! Based on these figures alone one can conclude that the average American is accustomed to a standard of living thirty times higher than that of the average Korean. Is this difference irreducible? In some respects, yes; in many others, no.

Particular attention must be given to two elements — food and protection against the cold. Once these elements have been provided for, it is remarkable how far one can go without endangering in the least physical or psychological health.

One thing an American has going for him is the fact that the people of Africa, Asia, and Latin-America know how Americans are accustomed to live. They see American movies, read our magazines, look at our television programs, and very often, come into contact with American troops and overseas government personnel. They know that an American casually takes for granted a million and one creature comforts which their flesh will never be heir to. Nor do they *expect* the American to live exactly as they do.

With these points in mind, let me give a concrete example of an American priest whom I know here in Korea who made a more or less successful effort in this direction. The priest whom I shall call "Father Jackson" was pastor of a parish located in a large urban slum area. One day, without saying anything to anyone, Father Jackson moved out of his simple, three-room rectory into a dilapidated squatter's shack which had been previously erected on church property and had since been vacated. Father found the going a bit rough at first. Rats had to be fought off and a battle with the elements, especially the cold and the rain, had to be won. Once these initial difficulties were overcome, however, Father Jackson discovered that his quarters were really quite pleasant. What is more, his health did not suffer in the least. Although Father did his own cooking, he was careful to provide a diet which was simple but, at the same time, adequate; he also made sure that the house was properly heated in winter. Father Jackson lived in his rectory-hut for four years and, when assigned elsewhere, he was really sorry to leave.

Moreover, this simple gesture on his part effectively served as sign and witness. It said something to both the people of the parish and also the priests of the diocese. The people and the priests did not necessarily like what it said but this is another point. As a matter of fact, the initial reaction of the parish bordered on hysteria. The people rushed to the pastor and shrilly protested that his rectory was a disgrace not only to the parish but to the diocese as well and, for that matter, to the entire Church of Korea. Since Father Jackson's shack was, if anything, *better* than the average dwelling in the area, he failed to grasp the logic behind his parishioners' arguments. He tried to reason with them, pointing out that Jesus himself lived in a stable and died on a cross stripped of all possessions. The parishioners, it seemed, had no objection to Jesus' living poor; but they did not want their pastor to live poor. After all, what would the Catholics in the parishes think? The priests of the diocese reacted with considerably more restraint. All they could think of to say was: "Why don't you do like everybody else?" These events took place when Father Jackson first made his move. When he moved out four years later, many of the people of the parish had begun to understand what it was all about.

In concluding this chapter a note of warning should be sounded. There is inherent danger for anyone — be he priest or layman — who goes against or outside the existing current. There is an implicit, subtle temptation to pride awaiting anyone who sets himself apart from his group by his life, by his words, or by his actions. Especially is this true in the area of material poverty.

If one lives poor while everyone else is living rich, his very life — whether he lives it or not — is a reproach to others. In this situation, it is so easy to become a bitter, self-righteous, finger-wagging reformer. This of course would be fatal.

No one accepts a proud truth. So, too, witness to poverty, if it is to be effective and authentically Christian, must at the same time be meek and humble. It must always be accompanied by a healthy sense of humor and a sense of the absurd. When one makes a fetish of poverty, or begins wearing his poverty as a badge, he is in trouble. May the Good Lord deliver us always from reformers who do not know how to laugh, who take themselves too seriously, and who nurse in their breasts a hard, gem-like flame which burns and burns and is never extinguished!

CHAPTER X

Christ's Presence in the Poor

Christ lives on in the world today and exerts his influence upon it *primarily* in four distinct ways: the Eucharist, Sacred Scripture, the Magisterium of the Church, and the person of the poor. If we believe in Christ we must at the same time accept his living presence in the Bread, the Book, the Church, and the poor.

He who made us dwells among us. He can be found not only in the silence of our tabernacles and in the solemn language of our sacred books, but also on our streets and in our market places. The living Christ is as close to us as the nearest poor person.

We see the mystery of the divine indwelling of the poor fore-shadowed in the Old Testament. Approximately one third of the Psalms revolve about the theme of man's poverty and suffering. With lyric tenderness, the psalmist expresses the nearness of God to those who are the most needy, the most helpless, and the most suffering.

The prophets also were inspired to associate themselves in a special way with the poor. Their mission was twofold: 1) to announce the word of God to the children of men, and 2) to defend the rights of the poor in the face of unjust aggressors.

Christ who came not to destroy but to perfect the law and the prophets not only associates himself with the poor, he identifies himself with them. Christ proclaims this truth in a most

solemn way in the 25th chapter of St. Matthew. This passage
is considered most important by St. Matthew because he places
it at the end of the last of the five great sermons which form
the framework of his Gospel. Christ is speaking here of the final
judgment and he concludes as follows: "Then the King will say
to those who are on his right hand, come you that have received
the blessing from my Father, take possession of the kingdom
which has been prepared for you since the foundation of the
world: for I was hungry and you gave me food, thirsty and you
gave me drink, I was a stranger and you brought me home, naked
and you clothed me, sick and you cared for me, a prisoner and
you came to me. Whereupon the just will answer: Lord when
was it that we saw thee hungry and fed thee, or thirsty and gave
thee drink; when was it that we saw thee a stranger and brought
thee home, or naked and clothed thee; when was it that we saw
thee sick or in prison and came to thee?' And the King will
answer them: 'Believe me, when you did it to one of the least of
my brothers here you did it for me.' "

Christ's choice of language in this passage is remarkably
similar to that which he used when he instituted the sacrament of
the Eucharist, and again, to that he used when speaking of his
Church. On the night before he died, Christ took bread, blessed,
broke, and gave it to his disciples, saying: "Take and eat. This is
my body." In like manner, he took wine and said: "This is my
blood." Before the Last Supper, the bread and the wine were one
thing; Christ another. Now they are one and the same.

A similar identification exists between Christ and his Church.
For example, as Paul lay bruised and shaken in the desert sand
on the road to Damascus Christ appeared to him and said:
"Saul, Saul, why dost thou persecute *me*?" Another example is
the words of identification Christ used in reference to his
apostles, the leaders of his Church, when he said: "Whosoever
gives a cup of cold water to one of these does it to me."

In much the same language Christ speaks of his presence in
the poor. He says: "As long as you did it to one of these, you did

it to me." Here again, the meaning is clear: whereas before the poor were one thing and Christ another, now they are one and the same.

Throughout the history of the Church, the saints, with that penetrating insight which characterized them, always saw Christ in the person of the poor. In reading the biographies of the saints, one frequently comes upon episodes in which personal contact with Christ is made through an encounter with a poor man.

A typical episode is that which is related in the life of St. Martin of Tours. On a cold wintry night, Martin of Tours was returning to Amiens on horseback. A half-frozen beggar appeared from nowhere and asked for alms in the name of Christ. Martin had nothing to give except his weapons and his clothes. So he rent his cloak in two, gave half to the beggar, and continued on his way. The following night, Christ appeared to him, clothed in the half-cloak which had been given to the beggar, and said: "Martin, the catechumen, has covered me with his garment."

An almost identical episode is recounted in the life of St. Catherine of Sienna. She exchanged her tunic for the tattered cloak of a beggar, and later on in a vision she beheld Christ clothed in the same garment which was now resplendent with jewels and precious stones.

St. John Chrysostom, another saint who probed the depths of the mystery of Christ's indwelling of the poor, said: "When the Church preaches to the poor it is Christ preaching to Christ." In a similar vein, he wrote: "Have you a desire to honor the body of Christ? Do not pass him by disdainfully when you see him naked and exposed to the shame of the street. Do not glorify him in the Church with garments of silk if you slight him without pity in the streets where he is perishing in cold and nakedness. For he who spoke the word of power, 'This is my body,' also said, 'I was hungry and you did not give to eat.' Show him the honor which he prescribed: give your riches to the poor."

The saints intuitively grasped the "supereminent dignity of the poor," as Bossuet once expressed it; and they felt themselves drawn and attracted to them. Blessed Albert of Poland, for example, chose to live among the human derelicts of Warsaw and to serve them as he would Christ himself. A Charles de Foucauld, living among the poor Tuareg tribes people in the wastes of the Sahara Desert, is another example. In our own day, we see an Abbé Pierre seeking out the rag-pickers of Paris, or a Mother Teresa seeking out the dying beggars of Calcutta, and ministering to them as a Mary of Bethany would minister to Christ. These people of God, searching for God, realize that he is not to be found in the clouds of heaven, but rather in the hovels of the poor.

Of course Christ is not present in the poor in the same way in which he is present in the Eucharist, Sacred Scripture, and his Church; but it does require the same faith to believe in this presence. It is easier to believe Christ present in an immaculate, richly ornate tabernacle, or to believe him present in words written on clean, germ-free pages, or again to believe him present in the impressive, solemn Magisterium of the Church, than to believe him present in the unwashed masses of poverty-stricken humanity. It requires faith of the deepest kind, a faith similar to that of the Centurion on Calvary. The Centurion looked up at the crushed figure of Christ upon the cross, a figure in whom there was neither beauty nor comeliness, and said: "Indeed, this was the son of God."

Or again, it requires a faith similar to that of the Magi, the three princes who left their pleasure palaces in Persia to follow a star. And the star led them to Bethlehem where they found a mother with a new-born child. The child in no way differed from other new-born children except for the fact that he was lying in a manger, but the Magi, upon seeing, fell down and adored.

The infinite God came to earth to beg two things of man — intellect and will, faith and love. What is more, he wanted these to be given freely with neither violence nor coercion. The Son of man could have cast himself down unhurt from the temple and forced the belief of the onlookers. He could have fed the crowds with loaves and fishes not once or twice, but every day in order to buy their love.

God, however, did not want to force belief nor to buy love. He wanted it given in humility and lowliness or he wanted it not at all. It was man's intellectual pride and willful arrogance which severed his relationship with God in the first place and it is this very pride and arrogance which man must swallow and destroy if he ever hopes to return to God.

So it is that the infinite God reveals himself to man through the most finite of finite things: the common, everyday substance of bread and wine; the simple words of human language; a child born in a stable and later on nailed to a tree; and the teeming masses of the poor who will always be with us. Man's heart must be permeated by humility if he is to come to God on such lowly terms. Such, however, is the law of the Incarnation and the economy of salvation.

For a Catholic, faith is the eucharistic presence, the inspired nature of Scripture, and the Magisterium of the Church comes early and easy. It is taught him at his mother's knee and is generally received without question. Faith, however, in Christ's presence in the poor comes much later and much harder. To many, it never comes. Yet, without this union through faith and charity with Christ in the poor, one's spiritual life will always remain stunted.

It is not sufficient merely to accept the poor on our own terms of human logic and rationalism. We must accept them on God's terms of faith and charity. Otherwise, they will always remain deadbeats, free-loaders, and parasites; they will never be Jesus of Nazareth.

For instance there is a knock at the rectory door, you open it, and a beggar, hat in hand, eyes downcast, asks for a handout. "You know how it is, Father. Things are tough all over. No work, no money; ain't had nothing to eat since yesterday." You draw back a step, look him up and down, try to get a whiff of his breath to see if he has been drinking, and attempt to trip him up with a sly question or two as he tells his story of hard luck and hard times. Then you try to pass the buck, "How about the Salvation Army, tried them? Or the Red Cross, sometimes they help fellows like you?" He persists. The old squeeze. So you reach down reluctantly in your pocket and give him a dollar, adding to it more than a dollar's worth of free advice. Then you close the door, and with a shrug of the shoulders say, "Well, guess I've been made a sucker of again."

And chances are you have. Not so much by the beggar, however, as by pride and common sense which keeps us from seeing and giving to Christ in the poor.

The story is told of an English scientist who stated that he would believe in the Eucharist only if he were permitted to take a consecrated host and examine it under a microscope. If, under the high-powered lens of his microscope, he could find some indication of a divine presence, then and only then, would he believe. If this were ever permitted the scientist, all he would see under his microscope would be the cell formation and chemical composition of bread. Unfortunately, a vision of the glory of God which can be received only through the eyes of faith would be denied him.

If we insist on putting the poor on glass slides to examine them with high-powered sociology and shiny reason, we will seldom see anything of God in them. We must continue to approach them with common sense, yes; but also with something of the nonsense and folly of faith.

Apart from all other consideration, the poor have a definite function in society and a clear role to play in the human community. They have been anointed by poverty to become mediators between man and God. Through them, men are permitted to sacrifice themselves to God and God in turn gives himself to men.

Christ's presence in the poor marvelously complements his presence in the Eucharist. In the Sacrament of the Eucharist, the Son of God gives himself to us in the form of bread, and we approach the table of the communion as spiritual beggars with outstretched hand and hungry heart. In "the sacrament of poverty" the roles are mysteriously reversed. Christ is now the beggar, and he humbly approaches us and pleads for bread.

Every theologian does not necessarily accept Christ's presence in the poor as Gospel truth. Far from it. This fact was brought home to me rather forcefully one day as I was accompanying a visiting Belgian theologian on a tour of the slums of Pusan.

As we were winding our way along a path which cuts and twists through the slum area it began to rain. We soon found ourselves ankle-deep in mud, slime, garbage, and human waste. The rain, however, in no way impeded the flow of life. Children continued to play in the slime; jiggey-carriers forced their way past us; hurrying people jostled us both from in front and from behind; others stared at us vacantly from the windows of their huts; chickens scurried about scratching in the mud; and dogs growled. The atmosphere of poverty closed in upon us as thick and oppressive as the fog which rolls in from the Bay of Pusan during the rainy season.

People here are forced to live on top of each other as a colony of rats. There is absolutely no privacy, no living space, no breathing space. Average *per capita* income in the area is around $75. There is no running water. No sanitation. No sewage disposal of any kind.

In this setting the theologian turned to me and said with much feeling: "It's absurd to say Christ indwells the poor. If this were so then we would be better off to leave these people as they are than to try to help them. If Christ is present in the poor then it follows that the poor man's poverty constitutes his dignity and we shouldn't do anything to disturb that. Really the whole idea is absurd."

Perhaps. But no more absurd than many other ideas in the Gospel. For example, what could be more absurd than the notion that God is present in a piece of bread?

One cannot say that Christ's presence in the poor either adds or subtracts anything to the intrinsic value of the poor man himself. Christ's indwelling is an outer-directed sign, a call to others for response, and a divine cry for pity and help. It is a sign very much like the outstretched hand of the beggar who asks us for alms.

One should view Christ's presence in the Eucharist in much the same way. Christ's physical indwelling of the bread does not really add nor subtract anything to its inherent dignity, nor to that of the tabernacle which shelters it. It should be looked upon as an outer-directed presence, a presence-for-others, a presence which cries out for response. The only presence which does add something to a person's intrinsic value is a divine presence based on faith and charity, and this is contingent on active consent to grace.

Christ's mere physical presence in Mary before the Nativity did not establish her essential dignity; rather, it was Mary's union with Christ through faith and charity which did. This is brought out in the Gospel narrative. When a woman in the the crowd cried out, "Blessed is the womb that bore you," Christ answered, "Rather blessed is he who hears the word of God and does it." Mary's union with Christ, then, is above all a free response to grace and was not contingent on Christ's mere bodily presence within her. If Christ's physical presence in Mary added something essential to her worth as a person, then one must conclude that after childbirth she was somehow less a person than before. This is simply not true. So too with the poor man. He is no less a person if he ceases to be poor and thus loses the outer-directed sign inherent in his poverty and need.

CHAPTER XI

The Final Judgment

Forty days after the birth of Jesus, when the days of Mary's purification were fulfilled, she took the child to the temple to present him to the Lord. A just and devout man by the name of Simeon entered the temple at the same time. He received the child from his mother, and blessing God, said: "Behold this child is destined for the fall and rise of many in Israel and for a sign that will be contradicted. And thy own soul a sword shall pierce."

The child did indeed grow up to become a sign of contradiction — a sign to be spoken against. Mary, too, shared in the contradiction meted out to her Son and her soul was pierced again and again by the tongues of his enemies.

The people of Palestine at the time of Christ judged themselves by their acceptance or rejection of the child whom Simeon held in his arms and who later presented himself as the Messiah. They and they alone determined their fate by their reaction to him. Those who recognized Christ as a sign of salvation were saved; those who saw in him only a sign of contradiction were condemned.

With Christ, moreover, there is no middle ground. He who is not with him is against him, and he who does not gather with him scatters. He who would prefer to remain lukewarm or indifferent is vomited out of his mouth.

Just as the person of Christ was destined for the fall and rise of many in Israel 2,000 years ago, so today the poor of the world are destined for our own rise or fall. Just as the people of Israel judged themselves by their attitude toward Christ, so today we determine our final judgment by our attitude towards the poor of the world.

In sum this is the meaning of the 25th chapter of St. Matthew where Christ placed our eternal judgment in the hand's of the poor. We have already seen the first part of this chapter; here let us consider its conclusion:

> "Then he will say to those on his left hand, 'Depart from me accursed ones into the everlasting fire which was prepared for the devil and his angels. For I was hungry and you did not give me to eat; I was thirsty and you gave me no drink; I was a stranger and you did not take me in; naked, and you did not clothe me; sick and in prison and you did not visit me.' Then they also will answer and say, 'Lord when did we see thee hungry and thirsty, or a stranger, or naked, or sick, or in prison and did not minister to thee?' Then he will answer them and say, 'Amen, I say to you, as long as you did not do it for one of these least ones you did not do it for me.' And these will go into everlasting punishment, but the just into everlasting light."

This same mystery is expressed in equally uncompromising language in the parable of Dives and Lazarus as recorded in the Gospel of St. Luke. It is a simple story of a have-not and a have-all and as such has profound meaning for our own day and age.

There was a certain rich man, clothed in purple and fine linen, who feasted everyday in splendid fashion. And there was a certain poor man named Lazarus, who lay at his gate covered with sores and who longed to be filled with the crumbs which fell from the rich man's table. And it came to pass that the poor man died and was borne away by angels to Abraham's bosom to enjoy there the good things which were denied him while on earth. But the rich man died also and was buried in hell to endure unspeakable pain and torment. The story ends with the rich man crying out to Lazarus for mercy. But the tables have been turned now and the cry of the rich man goes unheard.

It is important to note that the rich man in the parable is not necessarily condemned because he has much wealth or simply because he enjoys the good life. It is Lazarus, the poor man, who is the catalytic agent in the story. It is his presence at the rich man's gate which dramatically transforms his unshared wealth into something evil and something deserving of eternal damnation. As such, Lazarus becomes the symbol of all the have-nots of every time and every place who will rise up on the last day to point their finger in judgment at the Dives' of the world who are all uncaring, indifferent, can't-be-bothered haves.

It should be pointed out also that in both the parable of St. Matthew and again that of St. Luke the crime of the rich man is basically a crime of omission. In both instances the rich man does not *actively* seek to injure the poor, to insult him, or to rob him of his possessions. On the contrary, he sits back and does nothing. It is quite possible that Dives did not even know that a poor man, named Lazarus, was standing at his gate longing to be filled with the crumbs which fell from his table. But it is this very passivity, indifference, and reluctance to get involved which merit eternal damnation.

Belief that the last judgment has been entrusted to the poor of the world is an integral part of Christian tradition. For example, St. John Chrysostom wrote: "We should be grateful to the beggar who asks us for alms. We should fall down and kiss his feet; for he offers us eternal salvation." In a similar vein, St. Ambrose wrote: "Feed the man dying of hunger because if you have not fed him, you have killed him."

Let's have a look at the statistic which in this case can only be described as scandalous. The United States enjoys a Gross National Product of more than 700 billion dollars. Divide this by a population of 200 million and you get an average per capita American income of $3,500 a year. The average per capita income, however, in most undeveloped countries of Asia, Africa, and Latin America is $150. Since the income in these latter countries is distributed much more unevenly than in the United States, one can conclude that the average American citizen enjoys a standard of living at least 30 times higher than the average citizen of the third world of hunger.

How much of his 30 times greater income does the average American give in alms to the Lazaruses of the world? Again, let's have a look at the record. In 1948 at the height of the Marshal Plan we as a nation gave 2% of our GNP in foreign aid. Granted that this was given almost exclusively to Christian Europe, nevertheless it was *given*. Since 1948, however, there has been a slow but steady *decline* in foreign aid so that today we are giving only between one-third and one-fourth of 1% of our GNP in foreign aid. In other words, the average American is giving only about $10 out of his annual income of $3,500 to feed the Lazaruses of the world.

In one sense we are not even giving this, because we are getting more than this back from the underdeveloped nations in the form of trade, business, and industrial profits. There has been a 16% decline in the balance of trade during the last 10 years to the disadavantage of the have-not nations.

What is true in the area of finances is also true in the area of personnel. Each year, the United States sends many experts, technician, and engineers to aid the underdeveloped nations of the world, and we do this with a certain amount of publicity, fanfare, and trumpet-blowing. Fact is, however, the flow of experts across the waters in the other direction is even greater; that is, more native-born experts and intellectuals are coming from the underdeveloped nations to our shores than the number we are sending out. There is in fact a brain drain in the world and like everything else it is working to our advantage.

At the risk of sounding emotional let me present the situation in a somewhat different light. It is estimated that there are 24 million dogs in the United States and we as a nation spend 3 billion dollars each year to keep them fed, clothed, sheltered, doctored, groomed, manicured, and entertained. This figure exceeds what the United States spends on foreign aid. Not only is this true, but it can be stated also that with regards to food — both quantity and quality — shelter, playing area, living space, and medical treatment when sick, the average dog in the United States enjoys a higher standard of living than the average citizen of the third world of hunger of Asia, Africa, and Latin America. In the parable of St. Luke the rich man's dogs brought some small comfort and aid to the poor man by licking his wounds. One can not help but wonder what solace our pampered pets bring to the Lazaruses of today's world of hunger.

Pursuing the same line of reasoning, it is estimated that Americans spend more than 2 billion dollars a year on toys for their children — an average of $50 per family. A whopping 21 billion dollars more is spent annually on such luxuries as tobacco and alcohol. At the same time, the Food and Agriculture Organization estimates that each day between 10 and 12 million people in the world die of hunger.

As a nation, the U.S. grows richer at the rate of 4 or 5% a year — about 30 billion dollars annually. If, for one year, say, we were to earmark this increment for the poor of the world, we could completely eliminate hunger in a country the size of India. It should be noted that the suggestion here is not to sacrifice our already-accrued wealth, but merely for one year to resolve not to grow richer and fatter in order that some of the Lazaruses of the world may fill their bellies with the crumbs which fall from our table.

Another indicting fact in this discussion of our position via-a-vis the poor of the world is the glaring disproportion between what is spent on armament and that spent on food to feed the hungry. More than 70 billion dollars a year is spent for guns, while less than 3 billion is spent for bread to give to the poor of the world. Granted that all this is presented here in a rather black-and-white fashion; but so too was the case of the rich man in the parable of St. Matthew and again that of Dives in the parable of St. Luke. No doubt Christ could have thought up a number of mitigating circumstances to soften the impact of the stories; but he did not do so.

What is more, experts in the field state that the situation is not improving. If anything, it is getting worse. At the Vatican II Conference held recently at Notre Dame University and assisted at by such experts as Barbara Ward, Father Houtart, Monsignor Gremillon, James Norris, and others, the following blistering statement was issued: "The small, white, Christian and western minority are rich and growing richer by not less than 3% a year. Year by year, as their wealth increases, the attention, the investment, the aid they give the poor continents actually falls away. Each year, fewer crumbs fall from the rich man's table. This burning scandal makes a mockery of all pretensions to be a Christian and humane society."

One out of every six people in the world today may be classified as a Lazarus. In other words, he is starving. This means that his daily calorie intake is not sufficient to maintain normal activity without consequent loss of weight as the body begins to feed on itself. The actual number is about 500 million people.

In addition to this multitude of undernourished people, approximately twice this number, or 1 billion, suffer from *malnutrition*. That is, they have an improperly balanced diet and suffer from its inevitable effects on health and activity. The victim of malnutrition is prey to many protein-deficiency diseases such as dysentery, tuberculosis, rickets, anemia, and to numberless complications resulting from these conditions.

All this is but some indication of how we stand vis-a-vis our future judges, the poor of the world. In sum this is the teaching of the Second Vatican Council which in its *Constitution on the Church in the Modern World* declared: "Since the greater part of the world is still suffering from so much poverty it is as if Christ himself were crying out in these poor to beg the charity of the disciples."

"Some nations with a majority of citizens who are counted as Christians have an abundance of this world's goods, while others are deprived of the necessities of life and are tormented with hunger, disease, and every kind of misery. This situation must not be allowed to continue to the scandal of humanity."

CHAPTER XII

The World Is Sick

God has created all men equal. This does not mean that God gives all men equal talent, opportunity, and possessions but it does mean that he gives them the same dignity and the same destiny.

Man's dignity is that he has been created in the image and likeness of God. This unique dignity of man is first expressed in the account of creation in the Book of Genesis. God creates night and day, earth and sky, plants and animals with a mere pronouncement of his lips, a simple "Let there be this and let there be that." When it comes time for the creation of human life, however, God personally descends to Eden, takes clay from the banks of the river, and, as a sculptor, molds it into the form of man. God then bends over this inanimate lump of clay and breathes into it human life.

With every child after Adam God continues to breathe life into the clay or embryo formed by the union of man and woman. Human life, then, is a breath of the eternal living God. As such, it is something sacred, something which must be protected, nurtured, and permitted to fulfill the promise which it contains. Each new-born child whether he be born in the gutters of Calcutta, the slums of Rio de Janeiro, or a modern hospital in New York, has the same inherent and inviolable dignity.

He also has the same destiny. In the supernatural order, man's destiny is eternal life with God. In the natural order, it is self-fulfillment which is attained through the perfection of man's multiple talents and aptitudes.

This dignity and destiny which are the heritage of every man carry with them certain rights. Among the most basic of these are the right to food, shelter, clothing, and later on, the right to work and the right to marry. These rights, innate and God-given, form part of the natural law and as such can be neither ignored, denied, or violated.

God, who is author of these rights and who has created all men equal, has also created *all* the goods of the world for the use of *all* men, not for just a few.

God is like a mother who bakes a loaf of bread for her hungry children. There is enough for all, and the mother cheerfully invites her progeny to come and eat. The first child rushes in, cuts off a huge slice of the loaf, and greedily wolfs it down. A second child follows the example of the first and, between the two of them, four-fifths of the loaf disappears. Not much is left for the remaining seven or eight children. Some manage to get a few bites while others are left to satisfy their hunger with a piece of crust or with a few crumbs which have been left on the table.

The mother returns. She finds two of her youngsters with rosy cheeks and round bellies while the rest of her children stand around with pinched faces and empty stomachs. The mother is hurt and angry; not that she ever intended each child to have the same, exactly-measured portion; but she did hope that they would be a little fair about it.

Granted that the story is over-simplified; but, as we have already seen, so too is the present distribution of the world's wealth. Give or take a few percentage points, the fact remains that the United States with less than 6% of the population of the world possesses more than 40% of its wealth. Or to present it in another way, 15% of the population of the world who live in the North Atlantic community nations possess 80% of its wealth.

The Caucasian Christian nations of the North Atlantic Community have the lion's share of the loaf and they hold on to it tenaciously while Asia, Africa, and Latin-America are left to scramble for the crumbs. God has created a world sufficiently rich to nourish all who cling to her for subsistence; yet, as we have already noted, *at least* 1.5 billion people in the world are inadequately fed, clothed, and housed.

Moreover, for the first time in history, not only do we have enough food to feed all the people in the world, but what is equally important we have the means to transport it. We have the planes, the steamships, the railways, the trucks — and we have the know-how. We have the efficiency experts, the administrative geniuses, and the organization brains. Yet, with all this, at least one out of three people in the world remains either undernourished or malnourished.

We accept easily it seems the logic behind the moral principle which states that if my neighbor is starving, and I have bread, I must give some to him. I have the obligation to give my neighbor at least enough to maintain life. What is given, moreover, is given in justice not in charity. It is owed him, it is his due; and if I do not care to give it, he can come and take it and would be acting within his right.

This same simple logic seems to become blurred when projected on an international scale. The situation, however, remains basically the same.

One hundred years ago, my neighbor was he who lived in the same city or town as I. Then fifty years ago, with the advent of modern transportation, my neighbor became he who lived in the same country as I. Today, in this the last-third of the twentieth century when it takes an astronaut only 90 minutes to stroll around the world, my neighbor has become he who lives on the same planet.

At present, my neighbor, in the third world of hunger of Asia, Africa, and Latin-America, has nothing to eat. He has the right to ask for some of the bread which is on my table, and I have a concomitant obligation, not in charity but in justice, to give him a fair portion.

Such was the viewpoint of the Fathers of the Church who held that the aid which the rich man tenders the poor is not munificence but *retribution*. In other words, it is mere re-setting of the scales of justice and not something which depends on the voluntary generosity of one's heart. For example, St. Ambrose writes: "You are not making a gift of your possessions to the poor person, you are handing over to him what is his; for what has been given in common for the use of all, you have arrogated to yourself. The world is given to all and not only to the rich."

Most citizens of a rich nation like the United States find it difficult to accept this line of thought. Their reasoning runs in a different direction and may be summed up more or less as follows: "We, in America, have worked hard for what we have and we have no obligation to share it with anyone. Our fathers came to this land amid great hardships. They cleared the forests, fought off the savages, and, with their own toil and sweat, built up the colossus which is present-day America. As their descendants, we have a right to enjoy the fruits of their struggle. It is ours and we can do with it as we please."

This line of reasoning unconsciously flies in the face of a truth which we find repeatedly stated in the Bible; namely, all that man has and is except sin, comes from God. All is gift, all is grace. Our material wealth also must be viewed as coming from God, and God alone remains its absolute possessor. We are simply stewards of this wealth which we must dispense according to God's law and not according to our own selfish whim.

This doctrine is implicitly expressed in God's first instruction to Adam in the Garden of Eden. Adam understood that man governs the earth and all that is in it only as a caretaker, a custodian, a foreman who is employed by, and who must answer to, God. This doctrine is expressed again in the Book of Job. Job lost everything in one fell swoop — his crops, sheep, cattle, and his children — his reaction was basically an honest one. He did not shake his fists at the heavens as against a usurper; instead, the Bible says: "He shaved his head and fell down to the earth to do reverence. 'Naked I came,' said he, 'when I left my mother's womb, and whence I came naked I must go. The Lord gave, the Lord has taken away.'" St. Paul sums up all the arguments in one angry phrase which he flings in the face of man's pride: "O, man, what hast thou that you have not received!"

Most rich people effortlessly slip into a Calvinistic, pharisaical, or "Scrooge-like" view of prosperity and wealth. They tend to consider their riches as a sign of inherent superiority, a reward for virtue, hard work, and diligence, and a sure indication of God's favor and good pleasure. On the other hand, the poor are looked upon as inferior creatures who did not make the grade because of inherent weakness.

Because of the lopsided distribution of wealth in the world today Pope Paul, in his encyclical, *Progressio Populorum,* makes the flat-out statement: "The world is sick." Certainly, from the vantage point of the angels in heaven, the world must appear such. The picture of a fat, rich, opulent Western society in a lean, hungry, and starving world is clear indication that somewhere deep inside there is a major spiritual malady.

In America, people work eight hours a day in air-conditioned offices, come home to meals of steak and apple pie, watch TV at night, and in summer climb into expensive cars to motor to the seashore and mountains. The principal preoccupations of American society are relaxation, security, and enjoyment. One of its principal fears is obesity. The society is referred to by various writers as "the affluent society," "the leisure society," "the cosmetic society," and "the pleasure society." It has been written that the people of this culture measure their life out in coffee spoons and the monument to their generation will be a thousand lost golf balls.

In the third world of hunger of Asia, Africa, and Latin--America, the situation is dramatically different. For the vast majority of people in these areas, happiness is a full bowl of rice at meal time and a roof over one's head at bed time. The principal preoccupation of these people is: Where does the next meal come from? One of their principal fears is: What happens when I get sick?

In speaking of this contrast, an impoverished Korean student once remarked to me: "In America you ask yourself the question: how can I make my body thin? In Korea, we ask the question: how can I make my body fat? In America you wake in the morning and ask the question: how can I make my life more enjoyable today? In Korea, we wake in the morning and ask the question: how can I stay alive today?"

Christ came to earth, and walked and spoke and talked not as a philosopher or theologian but as a man of the people. He spoke the language of the people and they understood him; yet he always remained a mystic and, in a sense, a poet. When he looked at the world about him, for example, he did not see what other men saw. He saw a deeper, more hidden spiritual reality. When he saw the sky growing red and threatening a storm, he thought of the last judgment. When, on the road to Jerusalem, he came upon a withered fig tree, he was reminded of the spiritual barrenness of the Jewish people. When his gaze rested upon a field of golden wheat swaying in the breeze, he thought of the multitude of souls in the world ripe for the spiritual harvest which was in need of laborers.

If Christ, the poet and mystic, were to look about the world today and see its staggering social-economic imbalance, he would see this as an irrefutable sign that charity has grown cold and men have ceased to love one other. He would conclude that the world is possessed by the demon of greed and he would agree with Pope Paul that "the world is sick."

CHAPTER XIII

The Pope Is Sick

In his encyclical *On The Development of Nations* the Pope, as we have already seen, stated that "the world is sick." After release of his encyclical, *Human Life*, however, the tables were turned and the world began screaming that the Pope was the one who was really sick. Indeed, seldom has a single papal document caused such instant sound and fury, especially in the U.S., as did Pope Paul's July 25, 1968 statement on birth control. Because of its obvious relationship to the problem of population control and economic development the encyclical warrants at least some mention in a book of this nature.

Pope Paul in his encyclical does not ban birth control as such. What he teaches is that "each and every marriage act must remain open to the transmission of life." Mahatma Gandhi taught as much. So did the late "good" Pope John. So did all the Fathers of the Church.

Pope Paul, then, favors a family planning which respects the natural rhythms of fertility inscribed in the human body. These rhythms are independent of the will of man. To practice a family planning based exclusively on this cycle of nature is difficult. Pope Paul admits as much. But it is not impossible.

Proof that it is not impossible is that it has been and is being done. Countless married couples throughout the world have based their conjugal lives on these natural principles and have survived to tell about it. They speak of the discovery of a more noble more spiritual conjugal love. They also tell of the inner joy and peace which mysteriously flows from self-mastery and self-control.

Unfortunately, as the Pope alludes to in his encyclical, modern "aphrodisiac" society places man in an almost constant state of sexual tension. In such an atmosphere self-control becomes difficult and moral permissiveness becomes the order of the day. Accordingly, Pope Paul calls for a complete overhaul of social-sexual mores.

The results of the indiscriminate use of artificial birth control are there for all to see. The Pope mentions a few of these in *Human Life*: marital infidelity, sexual promiscuity, a general corrosion of the moral fiber, and a growing loss of respect for woman until she is gradually looked upon as a mere instrument of man's pleasure.

"First you lie," they say, "then you steal. Then you kill." First you practice artificial birth control. Then abortion. Then you say, what's the matter with pre-marital sex also? and why not a little homosexuality too just for a change of pace?

The rational arguments used by the Pope in his encyclical rest heavily on the concept of the natural law. The notion of a divine moral law inscribed in the heart of man which governs the flow and ebb of the forces of nature is an integral part of Catholic tradition; yet current confusion regarding this concept borders on the monumental. Although a full development of the subject doesn't fit into the scope of this chapter a concrete example drawn from history might be of use in throwing some light on the matter.

From what I have read the ancient Romans were very fond of orgies. All sorts of orgies — sex orgies, eating orgies, drinking orgies. Out of the eating and drinking orgies arose the classical institution known as the "vomitorium." The Roman gentlemen of yesteryear (so we are told) would sit down to a banquet, eat and drink to excess, then go to the vomitorium and throw it up. Then back to the banquet tables for a second round — and a third and a fourth.

This method of artificially extracting the sensual pleasure out of an act without at the same time assuming its natural consequences is obviously unnatural. This practice could be termed, if I may coin a phrase, artificial "contra-nutrition." An example of *natural* contra-nutrition may be seen in the practice of the modern calorie-counter who strives to get the most enjoyment out of the food while at the same time absorbing the least amount of fattening nutrition. Using reason and self-control the calorie-counter, however, goes about it in a way harmonious with nature. In no way does he do violence to nature by indulging, for example, in induced vomiting.

Analogies limp. So does the above. Still there is a valid parallel here between artificial contraception and artificial contra-nutrition. Both in greatly varying degree are a perversion of nature and in that same degree are a violation of the divine moral law.

Critics of *Human Life* have accused it among other things of being impossibly idealistic. When carefully considered, however, the tone and presentation of the encyclical message come across as strongly realistic, very human, and thoroughly Christian. As Christ in the Gospels, so, too, Pope Paul in his encyclical looks upon human weakness with compassion while at the same time holding high an ideal towards which "all men of good will" are invited to strive. The document itself is singularly devoid of anathemas, excommunications, and summary condemnations to hell for those who refuse to accept what it teaches. As a matter of fact the word "sin" is mentioned but once in the entire 6,000 word document.

What Pope Paul asks of men in his encyclical is basically what Christ asks of his disciples in every page of the Gospels, namely, good will and effort. In essence the Pope says: "Accept this doctrine in your heart as a divine truth and although it may demand sacrifice of you *try* to live up to it. If you fail, however, instead of being discouraged have recourse to the sacraments and continue to *try*."

In the Gospels Christ says: "Be you perfect as your heavenly Father is perfect." And again: "As I have loved you, so, too, must you love one another." What could be more idealistic than this! We must be perfect as God the Father and we must love as God the Son loved us. Yet Christ was addressing these words not to the angels in heaven but to flesh and blood creatures whose names were Peter, James, and John, and the other apostles and who on occasion could be just as petty and cowardly as any other son of Adam.

Today many are threatening to leave the Church because of her position on birth control. But this is nothing new. A similar phenomenon occurred in Christ's day when he first announced his doctrine on the Eucharist. Many of his disciples shook their heads and said, "This is a hard saying"—and began to walk away. Although Christ was certainly sorry to see them go, he did nothing to water down his doctrine to make it more palatable to them. He didn't even take a survey to see if his was the majority opinion or not. Instead he turned to Peter, the first Pope, and said, "Will you go away also?"

A similar episode occurred when Christ first announced his doctrine on marriage. The apostles found this, too, a bit hard to take and said: "If the case of a man with his wife is so, it is better not to marry." And Christ said: "Not all can accept this teaching; but to those to whom it has been given. . . . Let him accept it who can."

The Church is not a political party which hammers out a platform based largely on popular opinion polls. The Church with all its faults and weaknesses seeks out the will of God and presents it as she sees it with the single comment: "Let him accept it who can."

As a matter of fact, the majority of Catholic couples today in Europe and America do practice some form of artificial birth control. Some writers estimate the actual number to be 75%; still others put it as high as 90%. But this in no way makes the practice right, moral, licit, and good.

In a somewhat similar vein, youth counselors estimate that the majority of adolescent boys at some time or other practice masturbation. So what attitude should the Church adopt? Simply shrug her shoulders and say, "Boys will be boys," and let it go at that?

The Church, however, quietly continues to teach that the pure of heart are blessed and masturbation is wrong. Indeed, she can do no otherwise; for this is the natural law as she sees it in the light of faith and as preserved by a constant tradition. However, as in the case of artificial birth control or "mutual masturbation" as George Bernard Shaw once put it, so too in the case of masturbation, the Church does not fulminate and scream "mortal sin" at every failure. Instead she holds up high to men of good will an ideal and calls for a constant tension towards it.

Opponents of the encyclical are fond of presenting arguments based on so-called "humanitarian" reasons; and they are prone to describe in detail "countless millions in underdeveloped countries who will experience untold anguish because of it." Admittedly the problem takes on added dimensions when studied in the light of the population explosion now taking place in third world countries.

However, no encyclical is an "island sufficient unto itself, and *Human Life* is not meant to be read alone as an isolated document. It should be read in conjunction with *On the Development of Nations* in order to understand the Church's overall position on the problem of world poverty and overpopulation. When taken together the two encyclicals present a doctrine which is a marvel of ethical beauty, balance, and power. The encyclical *On the Development of Nations* teaches us that God has created a world sufficiently rich to nourish all who cling to her for subsistence. Yet God has created all the goods of the world for the use of all men, not for just a few. He didn't for instance, create a world in which he intended 15% of the population of the world to control more than 80% of its wealth — as is now the case. The problem, then, is not necessarily one of too many people; but rather of too many *selfish* people.

As has already been touched upon in the preceding chapter, for the first time in history not only do we have enough food to feed all the people in the world, but what is equally important we have the means to transport it. Yet people will insist that the only solution to poverty and over-population is global artificial birth control. If the world would use its wealth according to the principles enunciated in *On the Development of Nations* and practice a natural family planning according to the the guidelines of *Human Life* the population explosion could easily be defused and eventually be downgraded to something of a dud.

CHAPTER XIV

Individual Responsibility

Christ is the starved man stretched upon the cross of the world's poverty and pain. In essence this theme was developed in several preceding chapters. The question to be examined here is: What is this to me and to you? In other words, what is the personal responsibility of the individual Christian towards the poor of the world?

Everyone seems agreed that to effect deep lasting change individual charity is not enough. For this, international social and economic structures must be completely overhauled as well. Although individual charity may not be enough, at least it is a step, a start, a striking out in the right direction — and this is infinitely better than merely wringing one's hands or rending one's garments. This important point is forcefully made in the following passage excerpted from the encyclical *On The Development of Nations*:

> " 'If a brother or a sister be naked,' says St. James, 'if they lack their daily nourishment and one of you says to them "go in peace, be warm and be filled" without giving them what is necessary for the body, what good does it do?' Today, no one can be ignorant any longer of the fact that in whole continents countless men and women are ravished by hunger, countless numbers of children are undernourished so that many of them die in infancy, while the physical growth and

mental development of many others are retarded, and, as a result, whole regions are condemned to depressing despondency.

"Anguished appeals have already been sounded in the past . . . neither the private nor public funds that have been invested, nor the gifts and loans that have been made can suffice. It is not just a matter of eliminating hunger nor even of reducing poverty. The struggle against destitution, though urgent and necessary, is not enough. It is a question, rather of building a world where every man, no matter what his race, religion, or nationality, can live a fully human life, freed from servitude imposed on him by other men or by natural forces over which he has not sufficient control, a world where freedom is not an empty word and where the poor man, Lazarus, can sit down at the same table with the rich man. This demands great generosity, much sacrifice, and unceasing effort on the part of the rich man. Let each one examine his conscience, a conscience that conveys a new message for our times. Is he prepared to support out of his own pocket works and undertakings organized in favor of the most destitute? Is he ready to pay higher taxes so that the public authorities can intensify their efforts in favor of development? Is he ready to pay a higher price for imported goods so that the producer may be more justly rewarded? Or to leave his country, if necessary, if he is young in order to assist in this development of the young nations?"

Some people feel that because they can do little to change the world of poverty as such, or to lift up the mass of the poor as a mass, they are relieved of any responsibility to do something on an individual person-to-person basis. Such an attitude is hardly in keeping with the spirit of the Gospels.

Christ does not indwell the masses of the poor as a group or collectivity; rather, he is present in the heart of each individual poor man. Christ does not say, "As long as you did it to *these* you did it to me," but "As long as you did it to *one* of these the least of my brothers you did it to me."

The person who reasons that it is necessary to help *all* or *none* may be compared to someone with a life-belt in his hand standing on the shore of a storm-driven sea in which a million people are struggling to keep their heads above water. Overwhelmed by the knowledge that he cannot save the entire million, or even a significant fraction thereof, he drops the life-belt, turns his back on the sea of drowning individuals, and decides to wait. He decides to wait until the heads of state and the spiritual leaders of the world draw up a master plan to dry up the sea and permit the entire million people to walk safely to shore.

Christ himself was not intent so much on changing social-economic structures *per se* as he was on changing the hearts of individual men. For example, human slavery was a flourishing institution at the time of Christ yet neither Christ nor his apostles attacked it head on. Instead, Christ and his apostles devoted their energy to the changing of individual hearts and minds until finally, after several centuries, the walls of slavery came tumbling down. Economic slavery today is every bit as degrading as human slavery was 2,000 years ago. Its change, too, will be effected mainly through the transformation of individual hearts which in turn is possible only through charity.

In the Canticle of Canticles, it is written that "Charity is strong as death. It is like a flame, a flame of Yahweh. Muddy waters will not quench it, nor will rivers submerge it." Again, in the Epistle of St. John, we read: "He who abides in charity abides in God and God in him." Charity is a divine, infinitely dynamic force which is at man's disposal to transform the world and renew the face of the earth.

Here it is well to note that there is but one charity, one love in the world: the love of man for God joins and dissolves in the love of man for man. "For," in the words of St. John, "if a man says that he loves God, whom he does not see, and hates his neighbor, whom he sees, that man is a liar."

Precisely who is this neighbor of mine whom I must love? This question, first asked 2,000 years ago in Palestine, is of paramount importance because eternal life hinges on its answer.

A certain lawyer, got up to test Christ, saying, "Master what must I do to gain eternal life?" Jesus answered that he must love his neighbor. The lawyer, wishing to justify himself, said to Jesus, "And who is my neighbor?" The anwser to this question was given in parable form.

Christ chose a Samaritan and a Jew as the main characters of the parable with the role of hero going to the Samaritan. The Samaritans were as different from the Jews as night from day and they cordially hated one another. In the parable, the Jew is contrasted with the Samaritan and as such he represents the stranger and the foreigner. He is a symbol of everyone whose skin and tongue is different from mine, of him who lives across the waters and beyond the seas. His name is "every man," and the great lesson of the parable is, that he is my neighbor and my brother.

The implications of the parable are staggering. Christ in effect tells us that if, at present, there are 3 billion 500 million people in the world, then my neighbor and my brother, and he whom I must love in order to obtain eternal life is 3 billion 500 million minus 1.

In his First Epistle, St. John writes: "In this we have known the charity of God that he laid down his life for us. We ought to lay down our life for the brethren. He who has the goods of this world and sees his brother in need and closes his heart to him, how can he say the love of God is in him? My little children, let us not love in word and in tongue, but in truth and in action."

St. John has been called the mystic writer and at times born on the wings of the spirit he soars to transcendent, spiritual heights. At the same time, however, as seen in the preceding passage, his feet are planted on mother earth and he is solidly rooted in reality. St. John in essence says that love of neighbor does not consist in pious feelings of togetherness or in lovely words about the brotherhood of men, but rather in *doing* and in *giving*. Love is effectively expressed only by giving and convincingly proved only by doing.

One must be willing to lay down his life for his brothers. This does not mean, however, that all one has to do is sit patiently at his banquet table and wait for the glory of martyrdom to be presented him as his own severed head upon a silver platter.

Implied in St. John's words is the psychological fact that man tends to be identified with what he has and he tends to become one with what he possesses. When man gives of his possessions, then, he is giving of himself. When he distributes what he has to his neighbor he is in a very real sense laying down his life for his brother.

Looking around at the 3 billion 500 million people minus 1 in the world who are included in the term "neighbor," I see that he is in desperate need. In Hong Kong, he is homeless; in Korea, he is jobless; in India, he is sick; in South America, he is hungry; in Africa, he is illiterate. Just as Christ laid down his life for me, I *too* must lay down my life for my neighbor. I must give of myself — first and foremost in the form of my possessions.

By possessions, I do not mean the old clothes in the attic, nor the newspapers in the basement, nor the cancelled stamps in the desk drawer. I mean mostly money. Nothing is so quickly given, so rapidly transferred, and represents such immediate power to transform hunger into contentment, sickness into health, ignorance into knowledge, and unemployment into jobs than that everyday, much-maligned, much-abused substance, money. It has been called many things — everything from "excrement of the devil" to "filthy lucre"; yet it can speak the language of Christian love and do so most eloquently, dramatically, and forcefully.

Some people object that the giving of one's possessions is at best a naïve approach to the problem of world poverty. They feel that individual charity to the poor does little, if anything, to alter the direction of lives. In fact, they dismiss the whole issue with a shrug of the shoulders and the off-hand remark, "What good would it do?"

The answer is, it would do immeasurable good — first and foremost to the one giving. The adage "it is more blessed to give than to receive" did not originate on Madison Avenue. It is a divinely revealed truth first uttered by Christ himself (Acts 20:35).

Almsgiving offers so many spiritual benefits to the one practicing it that in many ways it may be likened to the sacrament of Confession. In the 12th chapter of the Book of Tobias, for instance, we read: "For alms delivers from death and the same is that which purges away sin and makes to find mercy and life everlasting." Again, in the Book of Ecclesiastes we find these words: "As fire quenches water, so does almsgiving take away sin." Christ expressed a similar truth in the New Testament when he said to the Pharisees: "If you wish to be clean on the inside, sell what you possess and give alms to the poor." The same theme is expressed in the Epistle of St. Peter by the phrase: "Charity covers a multitude of sins." Charity to the poor, then, not only atones for sin; it takes away sin.

Granted, then, that almsgiving and individual charity brings immeasurable blessings to the one practicing it, what good can it do to the one receiving? Can it alter lives or change the direction of human existence? In many cases, it can and does.

In the third world countries where average annual income is under $150, an isolated donation of $10, say, can profoundly influence human life. Continued on a regular basis, such a donation can permanently and radically alter it. Let me illustrate the point with a few examples from the local Korean scene with which I am familiar.

Example. Agatha Han, age 41, widow, suffering from stomach cancer, 4 small children, no income, intends to place children in orphanage. A gift of $10 a month can prevent this and enable the family to stay together and survive as a family.

Example. Cho Il Sun, 32, crippled, beggar, lives with wife and younger brother and sister in a shanty. Needs a loan of $25 to set up a clothing stall in the Pusan market. The income would permit him and his family to live more or less as human beings.

Example. Pak Ou Tek, 17, parentless, shoe-shine boy, lives in a cave. Losing his hearing. Needs $50 for an ear operation which would not only relieve the pain of his affliction but also save his hearing.

Example. Lee Helena, 47, lives with husband and five children. Two other children sleep in a neighbor's house because there is not enough room in her hut for the whole family. Needs loan of $40 to build a large shack. A gift of this nature would radically change her life and that of her family.

One could go on and on *ad infinitum* with similar examples, but it is hardly necessary. The point is, charity to the poor even on an individual basis can effect profound good and even permanently alter the course of human life.

Another question which sometimes comes up is, how should one give? At present there are 11 thousand American priests, brothers, and sisters serving in Africa, Asia, and Latin America. One could channel his gift to the poor through any one of these or their representatives in the United States. Or through Catholic Relief Services. Or through the Society for the Propagation of the Faith. Or through any one of the hundreds of other American volunteer relief agencies now serving overseas. This question does not merit prolonged consideration. Once one is convinced of the need-to-give and is possessed of a will-to-give, a way-to-give can be easily found.

A final question concerning individual charity comes to mind, to what extent must I give? Is one-tenth enough? Must I give half of my possessions as did Zacchaeus in the Gospel story Or does Christ demand *all* as he did of the rich young man in the Gospel of St. Mark? This is for each to decide in the forum of his own conscience; nevertheless, one or two general guidelines may be of some value here.

As one's wealth increases, his standard of living should remain more or less the same. At the same time, the standard of living of Christ in the person of the poor should improve. More money should not mean more personal pleasure, security, or prestige. It should mean that one now has more power to serve, more to give to Christ in the poor, and, in the final analysis, more to invest in eternal happiness.

For example. A young couple starts off in life, not with an expensive ranch-style home in the suburbs, but rather with a modest six-room house in a poor section of the city. Furnishings include all the necessities; but they do not include stereo, electric dishwasher, deep freeze, air-conditioner, wall-to-wall carpeting, and so on. For transportation, the couple uses a Volkswagen. Food, although wholesome and adequate, is mostly of the hamburger-meat loaf variety. As time goes by, promotions come, wages increase, and more money flows in. But, except for necessary minor adjustments, the basic standard of living of the couple does not radically change. The standard of living of a poor family in Pusan and another in Calcutta does — because they are the recipients of the alms given by the couple. These families are now able to eat and be clothed and sheltered as befits human beings. At the same time, the temporal health and happiness of the young couple in the example are in no way affected. Their eternal health and happiness, however, are immensely affected — to the good, of course.

St. Paul in his writings tells us that the disciple of Christ should aspire after the simple life and tend, as much as possible, to eliminate unnecessary frills and extras. For example, in his Letter to Timothy, he writes: "For we brought nothing into this world and certainly we can carry nothing out. But having food and wherewith to be covered, with these we are content." St. Paul makes little allowance here for luxuries.

But what is a luxury and what is a necessity — and who is to judge the difference between the two? The answer is, the poor of the world. Since Christ placed our final judgment in the hands of the poor we should get in the habit now of looking at our use of money with their eyes; and we should submit every decision of the luxury-necessity type to their hard scrutiny. A trip to Europe, a summer cottage by the seashore, a new car, a yacht, an expensive pet, a visit to the beauty parlor — luxury or necessity? The criterion is, how would the Lazaruses of the world, covered with sores and longing to fill their bellies with the crumbs which fall from our tables, look upon it?

Some people seek refuge in Scripture in an effort to flee their responsibility towards the poor of the world. They simply repeat the words of Christ, "The poor you will always have with you," and then go on their merry way.

Such people remind one of St. Paul's observation that even Satan can make use of Scripture to "prove" that God does not exist. While these people do not try to disprove the existence of God they unwittingly try to disprove the existence of a God of love which is just as reprehensible.

The above quotation is used to such simplistic fashion that one is tempted to ignore it altogether. However, it is used with such disconcerting frequency and occurs in so many unexpected places that it can not be passed over in silence. For example, when Mr. Sargent Shriver, the former U.S. Director of the War on Poverty, paid a visit to Pope Paul, he asked the Holy Father to explain the precise meaning of this text. Mr. Shriver said that so many people used the text as a club against him that he needed good arguments for defense.

This quotation, taken from the Gospel of St. Matthew, must be understood in the context in which it was spoken. Mary of Bethany had just performed a sacred, symbolic act: she had anointed Christ with precious ointment in preparation for his burial. Judas Escariot reproached her for this act of love by pointing out that the ointment could have been sold and the money given to the poor. Not that he cared about the poor, but he held the purse strings — and he was a thief. Christ defended Mary's action by quoting a text from the Book of Deuteronomy (XV, 11) which begins with the words: "The needy will never be lacking in the land." This part appears in the Gospel, but the text from Deuteronomy continues: "This is why I command you to open your hand to your brother, to him who is humiliated and poor in your land." In other words, the very text which people cite as an argument *against* helping the poor really forms part of a command from God to assist them.

Moreover, Christ uses the phrase purely as a statement of fact. He does not say that it is a *good* thing that the poor will always be with us; or that one should be resigned to the fact that the poor are always with us; or that one should actively see to it that the poor will always remain with us. On the contrary, Christ is simply and passively referring to a fact of human existence. He could just as easily have said, "Children will always be with you"; "The sick you will always have with you"; or "Sinners you will always have with you"— because that's the way things are; not necessarily the way things *should* be.

A twisted interpretation of one isolated text of the New Testament is certainly a weak justification for personal indifference to the poor of the world. Those who hide behind this text can test the accuracy of their scriptural exegesis at the last Judgment when Christ says to them: "I was hungry and you did not give me to eat." They can answer: "But Lord, did you not say 'The poor you will always have with you?'"

CHAPTER XV

Foreign Aid Disillusionment

Time was when foreign aid was the fair haired child of both the liberal and the conservative. Such is no longer the case. Yesterday's child with the golden hair has turned into today's favorite whipping boy.

Eric Schumacher, a noted British economist, in a recent address to the Africa Bureau, summed up the situation well when he said: "The unprejudiced observer, who does not spin theories but simply takes in what he sees, notices increasing desperation among the great majority of people who, in many places, are making no progress at all. The impartial observer cannot help noticing, also, that most of the so-called developing countries are plagued by large-scale and increasing unemployment. If the proverbial visitor from another planet would come and have a look he might say, "I do see development but little improvement; I do see great changes, but no signs of growing economic health. I hear a great deal of talk about approaching the take-off point, but I see it receding. I notice more and more countries requiring ever-increasing food imports; I see increasing balance-of-payments problems — not increasing stabilization on the economic front." And he might also say that he sees increasing political instability.

"Turning his attention to the aid-giving world he will undoubtedly say 'I see increasing disillusionment.' A few years ago, one could say that only a kind of lunatic fringe in the aid-giving countries was openly critical of aid, and even against it. But today, this is no longer so. Disillusion is spreading fast."

Another typical example of this "disillusion" to which Mr. Schumacher refers — this time taken from the grass roots level — can be seen in the following "Question Box" answer which appeared recently in a Catholic diocesan newspaper.

> *Question*: Isn't it sinful to spend billions of dollars on space projects when millions of people in the world do not have the necessities of life?
>
> *Answer*: No, it would first have to be proved that the money spent is a waste, bearing no reward except the satisfaction of idle curiosity or vanity and that the money thus saved would certainly relieve the extreme needs of the world's poor. Neither is true, of course. Although nations, like individuals, have a duty to help other nations when possible, their first duty is to themselves. Since the needs of the world's poor are not extreme but only grave, and since it is by no means certain that foreign aid always brings proportionate benefits this expenditure has to be regulated by the ordinary demands of prudence. It is naïve to think that millions of American dollars in foreign aid ever actually benefited the poor.

In order for any given third world nation to escape from poverty into the sunlight of economic prosperity two things are required; the first is foreign aid; and the second is the education and discipline necessary to make it work. One without the other is incomplete and will achieve at best only very limited results.

A few examples come to mind. After the war, the economies of both Japan and Germany were reduced to rubble and ruin. They were every bit as depressed then as the most depressed of the so-called "emerging" nations today. In the space of two decades, however, both Japan and Germany, achieved economic "miracles" which are the admiration of the world. Actually, these "miracles" lose something of their glitter when one considers that both Japan and Germany's education and disciplinary substructure were left intact by the war. All they had to do to achieve their "miracle" was to re-build on this foundation with of course the necessary outside help. A nations' internal education and discipline may be compared to the 7/8's of an iceberg which remains submerged and out of sight. The 1/8 which rises above the surface for all to see and admire is a nation's capital investment and technological, industrial complex.

Two other examples are Israel and Hong Kong. Neither of these countries has much to boast about in the way of natural wealth or resources. Yet, because of proper organization, motivation, and discipline, they have managed to build up stable and independent economies.

Examples of the contrary proliferate. One which immediately comes to mind is that of Brazil. Of Brazil, it has been said: "It is the country of the future and will always remain so." Brazil is fantastically wealthy in natural resources but, because of some fatal flaw in its national chemistry, it has never been able to exploit them properly.

Many of the Middle East Arab nations also may be pointed to as classic examples of what shouldn't be done. For years they have been pumping oil from their deserts and all but drowning in fact, foreign royalties. Yet their economies as a whole have never taken off. In fact, they seem every bit as impoverished today as they ever were. One reason for this state of affairs seems to be a serious lack of ethical discipline, social consciousness, and foward-looking education — all of which are indispensable elements in the prosperity equation of any nation.

The corruption running through all levels of society in most have-not nations has become legendary and at times seems to reach heroic proportion. Nor is it accurate to think that the situation is overblown. Anyone who has had long-term first-hand and in-depth contact with these countries will state that, if anything, the situation is *under*estimated.

One cannot simply shrug off this corruption as the natural outgrowth of poverty and say that *mutatis mutandis* the same conditions prevail everywhere — even in the West. They do and they don't. The similarity is, perhaps, 25%; the dissimilarity, 75%. A person suffering from acid indigestion can be likened to someone afflicted with stomach cancer because both are sick with a belly ache. In the same sense, the corruption in many third world countries can be compared to that in the West.

The Church could and should render inestimable service to third world countries precisely in this area of education and discipline. In too many instances, however, the Church herself has seriously compromised her position and, in so doing, has forfeited any right she might have had to be a sign of justice, honesty, and integrity.

An example of a typical third world country — let's call it "Wollam"— will help to prove my point. Since 1945, Wollam has received more than 4 billion dollars in foreign aid and capital assistance. If this money had been used with a minimum flair for social justice and the common good, the country today would be on an economic par with Japan or Israel. Such is not the case.

Too much of Wollam's foreign aid dissolved and disappeared in graft and corruption. Much more was devoted to prestige and political projects whose primary purpose was to dazzle rather than to build up a stable economy. The actual amount which in time trickled down to the man in the street has been disappointingly small. Twenty years have gone by since the first foreign aid started into Wollam but the economy is still nothing to dance in the streets about. According to a recent government survey, 70% of the working population still subsist on salaries of $22 a month or less; the average farm income is still only $100 a year; and the cost of living has risen 40% in the last five years. Wollam's economy has improved as a whole but it is mostly a question of a handful of the rich getting much richer and the masses of the poor getting a little better.

How about the Church in Wollam? What has her position been during this crucial period? Overly preoccupied with institutions and structures, overly-concerned about prestige, power, and measurable results, the Church, too often, has been guilty of avarice, deception, smuggling, black-marketeering, tax-evasion, and outright defrauding of the poor. Outside of the government, the Church today is the richest single institution and biggest property holder in all of Wollam. Nothing is the matter with wealth and property if it is used to serve the poor, but more often than not the Church in Wollam has used it for its own glory and that of the rich and middle class.

Some of the Church's wealth accrued from the frenetic land grab which ensued after Wollam's former occupiers were expelled. Much more came from illicit trafficking in relief funds and relief goods. Often the Church took the bread of the poor and either bartered with it, or sold it outright to build up her cherished brick and mortar structures. Of 21 churches constructed during the last twenty years in a major city of Wollam, 14 have been built in whole or in part by defrauding the poor in one way or another of their patrimony. Moreover, in order to protect these acts, people in places high and low have had to be bribed, lies told, and documents falsified. The whole process from beginning to end has been morally and socially corrosive.

In many instances, the Church in Wollam has instigated outstanding social programs and charity projects, but more often than not the moving force behind these, has been the foreign-born missionary element — rather than the native-born Church herself. Also on occasion, the Church has issued stirring statements on social justice; but the powers that are and the people in high places are not so easily taken in. They know the Church for what she is and, since the Church has been guilty of dishonesty over a long period of time, they feel that she has lost the right to point her finger at anyone. For the Church in Wollam to recover her lost position she must undergo a thorough inner conversion which is always painful and humiliating. The Church must also begin to make massive restitution to the poor — which is even more painful and humiliating. From what I have heard and read, the situation of the Church in Wollam does not seem to differ dramatically from that of the Church in many other third world countries.

The role of the Church in both the world of the have-nots and the world of the have-alls, should resemble that of John the Baptist at the time of Christ. Of John the Baptist, Christ said: "What did you go out to the desert to see? A reed shaken by the wind? A man clothed in soft garments? But I tell you those clothed in soft garments and banqueting sumptuously are found in the houses of kings: I tell you you went out to see a prophet and more than a prophet." Clothed in camel skin and eating locusts and wild honey, John dwelt in the desert region beyond the Jordan and preached a penance based on social justice. He cried: "Brood of vipers, who has shown you to flee from the wrath which is to come: let he who has two tunics give to him who has none and let him who has something to eat do the same."

Indifferent to structures and institutions, the Church too must be a Church of the desert preaching a penance based on social justice. A Church of exodus and a Church of the second coming, she must shed her soft garments and flee the houses of kings. Her eyes burning with a vision of a new heaven and a new earth, she must rage against injustice and corruption wherever she finds it and whatever the consequence. As John the Baptist, and all the other prophets of old, she too must assume her role as defender of the weak and champion of the poor.

Such a Church in the West could be a marvelous stimulant to foreign aid and overseas assistance programs. She could effectively offset disenchantment with present-day programs and stir up desire to begin new ones. Such a Church in the third world areas which are on the receiving end of foreign aid, could be a sign of social justice, honesty, and integrity, and she could make a priceless contribution in the domain of ethical education and moral discipline. Accordingly, she could prepare a climate of social consciousness and awareness in which foreign aid could be effectively and productively employed.

6

CHAPTER XVI

Social Action and Contemplation

Man's attempt to help his fellow man very often achieves only mediocre results. At times it achieves nothing at all, or even worse, causes actual harm.

The distribution of free food — intended to relieve hunger — ends up by creating legions of permanent beggars which society is at a lost to cope with. The ambitious modern charity hospital — intended to relieve suffering and pain on a large scale — reduces infant mortality, prolongs life, and greatly contributes to the more serious social problem of overpopulation. The expensive orphanage — constructed and maintained with foreign funds — becomes an important contributing factor to child abandonment in urban slum areas. Old age homes — built with the best of intentions — end up by encouraging the young to neglect needy and aging parents. The direct grant of relief funds — designed to alleviate poverty — often leaves the poor man convinced that society owes him a living and in turn contributes to a general weakening of the social fabric.

To help one's fellow man on a strictly material level is not an overwhelming task. All that is required is to buy bread and give it to him. But to help man *integrally* — which means not only materially, but spiritually, psychologically, and emotionally as well — is infinitely more difficult. Man is incapable of assisting his fellow man on this exalted level unless God himself is called upon to intervene. The act of humility, then, which is prayer, is indispensable to meaningful Christian service of the poor.

The so-called "new morality" at work in the world today tends to exalt human effort and social action while at the same time making light of prayer and contemplation. Modern man seems slightly bored by talk of prayer. He is convinced that all can be accomplished by human effort alone, including the building up of the New Jerusalem in which all men will join hands and sing everyday in the sunshine of justice and brotherhood. Bible phrases such as, "Without Me you can do nothing," and "Unless the Lord build the house, those who build it labor in vain," sound hallow and irrelevant to the modern ear.

As a result of human intelligence man today reaches up to the stars, taps the ocean depths, splits the atom, and penetrates the heretofore secret regions of the human psyche. He eradicates disease, prolongs human life, invents machines which think and machines which talk. All this is praiseworthy and cause for rejoicing, but when it comes to helping a fellow human being in a really meaningful way man must admit that he is still a child.

The apostles, at the time of Jesus, tried by their own power to assist a fellow man who was a deaf mute possessed by a demon. Their efforts were in vain. Puzzled by their own failure they asked Christ the reason and he answered: "This kind can be cast out only by prayer." In the Acts of the Apostles, when St. Peter cured the cripple at the portico of the temple, he did so not in the name of human power but in the name of Jesus who alone has the power to heal and to save.

Christ's social action, as depicted in the Gospels, is usually in some way joined to prayer. For example, before Christ distributed the loaves and fishes to the multitude in the desert, he first lifted up his eyes to heaven and prayed. He also prayed when he called forth Lazarus from the tomb. Again, when Christ cured the man born blind, the paralytic by the pool, and the ten lepers, he did so in a prayerful, religious context.

Only through contemplation can man arrive at a clear vision

of what man is; and this is indispensable if one wishes to serve his fellow man in a meaningful way. In the light of contemplation, man is seen to be much more than the *"animal rationale"* or the *"homo sapiens"* of the philosophers. He is also seen to be the *"capax Dei"* of the mystics and the saints.

"Capax Dei" ("capable of God") is a description of man in his most sublime dimension. Poor little finite creature though he be, man is still able to be filled with God as a glass with wine or a room with sunlight. Man has within himself the capacity to become a child of God and to share fully in the divine life. Not just the rich man, nor the educated man, nor the man who happens to be a member of a North Atlantic community nation but *every man* has this capacity. Every man who can stand up straight and look at the stars has the same inherent potential to surpass himself and to reach out and embrace God.

The distance between man and God is beyond human imagination. It is the distance between the finite and the infinite, the creature and the created, the sinful saved and the sinless Savior. Yet by a mystery which will never be fully plumbed, this distance has been bridged and man has now "become as God." In a very real sense man is capable of knowing as God knows, loving as God loves, and sharing fully in the divine life.

To understand better what this means, a comparison from the animal world may help. Suppose, that by strange alchemy, one were able to give a cherished pet — a dog, say — a share in the human condition. As a result of the process, the dog would be able to speak, think, laugh, pray, and love as man. One would be dizzy with wonder at the sight of such a phenomenon; yet the distance between man and beast is negligible when compared to that which separates man from God.

Whenever one sets out to serve society, it should always be in light of this fundamental vision of man as "capax Dei." Otherwise, one's service will be short-sighted, short-lived, and, in the final analysis, short-circuited as well.

Pope Paul has warned against the dangers of a lesser vision

of man. He puts us on our guard against an overly materialist and naturalist view of man in his encyclical *"On the Development of Peoples"* in which he states the following:

> "Christ's teaching also applies to people: 'what does it profit a man to gain the whole world if he suffers the loss of his soul?'
>
> "Less well-off peoples can never be sufficiently on their guard against this temptation which comes to them from wealthy nations. For these nations all too often set an example of success in a highly technical and culturally developed civilization. They also provide the model for a way of acting that is principally aimed at the conquest of material prosperity. Not that material prosperity of itself precludes the activity of the human spirit. On the contrary the human spirit increasingly free of its bondage to creatures can be more easily drawn to the worship and contemplation of the Creator. However, modern civilization itself often complicates the approach to God not for any essential reason but because it is excessively engrossed in earthly affairs.
>
> Developing nations must know how to discriminate among those things that are held out to them. They must be able to assess critically and eliminate those deceptive goods which would only bring about a lowering of the human ideal and to accept those values that are sound and beneficial in order to develop them alongside of their own in accordance with their own genius.
>
> What must be aimed at is complete humanism, and what is that if not the fully-rounded development of the whole man and of all man? A humanism closed in on itself and not open to the values of the spirit and God who is their source could achieve apparent success. True, man can organize the world apart from God, but without God man can organize it in the end only to man's detriment and isolated humanism is an inhuman humanism. There is no true humanism but that

which is open to the absolute and is conscious of a vocation which gives human life its true meaning. Far from being the ultimate measure of all things, man can only realize himself by reaching beyond himself. As Pascal has said so well, "Man infinitely surpasses man."

Were it not for his exalted vision of what man is capable of, Christ's approach to the problem of poverty in his day could be judged quietistic and abstractionist. Although "all things were made through him and without him was made nothing that was made," Christ really did little to relieve directly and massively the material misery of the people among whom he lived. He healed a number of sick people, he raised three individuals from the dead; once he made wine from water, and, on two occasions, he multiplied a few loaves and fishes. These relatively isolated miracles were primarily signs of God's love and concern for men, and only secondarily were they intended to relieve a particular human distress. They always pointed to a hidden, spiritual reality and as such helped to reveal to man the meaning of his existence and show him the way to true self-fulfillment. For example, Christ's primary intention in raising Lazarus from the dead was to teach men that he was the source of true life, and only secondarily to bring one individual back from beyond the grave. Otherwise it can be said that Christ in a sense failed because Lazarus did die again — or at least one may reasonably presume so.

A priest's view of the role of works of charity in his general apostolate should be similar to that of Christ. He *should* begin relief programs, he *should* engage in social action and he *should* initiate economic reform but always after the manner in which Christ performed his miracles of service; namely, primarily as so many signs of God's love and concern for men. These signs, morever, should be relegated to a secondary role in order of importance. The main role of the priest, as that of Christ, remains the verbal proclamation of the Word of God.

As much as possible, works of charity undertaken by a priest should be small scale, well-contained, and as direct and personal as possible. For example, if one has a choice between building a large city hospital or a small neighborhood dispensary in the heart of the slums, he should opt for the latter. When any given social program becomes too big, too organized, too expensive or too impersonal, it inevitably tends to lose its value as a sign of God's love among men. By the same token it becomes indistinguishable from a money-making project, a prestige-oriented program, or a taken-for-granted, state-run, charity institution. Such a program often gives the impression to the man in the street of being surrounded by a general cure of wealth, power, and ambition which turns it into a countersign of the purpose for which it was established.

When Christ healed and helped in the Gospels, it was usually at close range and with his own two hands. For example, when he healed a deaf man, he made clay out of spittle and earth and inserted it with his own fingers into the man's ears. At Naim Christ placed his hand on the casket of the widow's son and commanded him to arise. Again, Christ took the daughter of Jairus by the hand and raised her to life. When Christ performed the greatest of his social miracles, the multiplication of the loaves and fishes, he took bread, broke, and began the distribution himself with his own hands.

As a general rule a priest should limit himself to small-scale person-to-person, face-to-face relief programs. By giving himself over completely, however, to the proclamation of the Word of God, he will inject into society a dynamism which will have consequences in the social-economic fields far surpassing what he himself could achieve by direct social action. The truth of Christ contains the seeds of a social revolution of cosmic proportion, and the priest's role is to sow these seeds in the heart of society. This is what St. Thomas Aquinas had in mind when he wrote: "The greatest charity is the giving of truth."

The apostles realized that they were not called primarily to be economists, social workers, or administrators, but rather prophets and men of prayer. Accordingly, they placed strict limitation on their social action. This problem arose early in the life of the Church and it is interesting to read in the Acts of the Apostles VI, 1-4 how it was resolved.

"Now in those days, as the number of the disciples was increasing, there arose a murmuring among the Hellenists against the Hebrews that the widows were being neglected in the daily ministration. So the Twelve called together the multitude of the disciples and said 'It is not desirable that we should forsake the Word of God and serve at tables; therefore, brethren, select from among you seven men of good reputation, full of the Spirit and wisdom, that we may put them in charge of this work. But we will devote ourselves to prayer and to the ministry of the Word.' "

It is often said that you cannot preach to people who are hungry. Nor can you expect people who are destitute to be concerned about God and their souls.

Granted that people who are hungry are not as receptive as people who are well-fed; nevertheless, they are capable both of hearing the Word of God and also of accepting it in their heart. One would be doing the poor an injustice by stating dogmatically that they are incapable of learning about God, praying, or grasping, in some manner at least, the eternal truths of salvation.

St. Thomas has said that a minimum of material goods is necessary to lead a good Christian life. This "minimum," however, varies with different people and different places. Moreover, even St. Thomas does not say that it is impossible to lead a less-than-perfect Christian life even without this minimum of material goods. People who are poor and hungry, perhaps, cannot go to Mass every day, nor study the catechism regularly, nor devote a daily half hour to spiritual reflection. Still, they are "capable of

God." In whatever condition man finds himself — sick, starving, or half-dead — he always remains "capable of God," capable of transcending himself and surpassing the human condition.

In the Gospel, Christ said: "Do not be concerned with what you shall eat or what you shall wear; for after all these things do the heathen seek. But seek first the kingdom of God and its justice and all these things will be given you besides." These strongly quietistic-sounding words were spoken to people who knew the meaning of day-to-day poverty, hunger, and insecurity. Yet, by these words, Christ clearly establishes priority: first, the kingdom of God and his justice; and second, food, clothing, and all those things after which the heathen seek. Social programs and relief projects, then, are always to be launched with a view of what man is, namely, one who is "capable of God" and his kingdom. Such a view comes only through prayer and contemplation.

CHAPTER XVII

Poverty in Reference to Service

In a previous chapter, we considered poverty in reference to Christ, the poor man. In this chapter we will consider it in relation to apostolate and service of the poor with whom Christ identifies himself.

In his own apostolate, St. Paul set for himself the good of becoming "Jew with the Jews, Greek with the Greeks, all things to all men in order to win them to Christ." In much the same manner, the disciple of Christ today aspires to be poor with the poor in order both to win them to Christ and to serve them more effectively.

Becoming poor with the poor should not be looked upon as something remarkable or extraordinary. It is but a simple application of the law of the Incarnation. According to this law, Christ became like unto man in all things except sin in order to redeem man. Christ came to earth to serve and to give his life as a ransom for many. He could have done this from afar without, in a sense, soiling his hands or bruising his body. He could have done it by a simple act of his will or a decree of his lips. But he did not choose the easy way. Instead, the Word "Who in the beginning was with God and was God" became flesh, dwelt among us, and, shared fully in the human condition with all its pain, humiliation, and death.

The mystery of the Incarnation reveals to us love in its most authentic form which implies identification and conformity with the one loved. In order to love the poor as Christ loved us, we must dwell among them, share fully their condition, and become like unto them in all things except sin.

One would find it difficult, for example, on a purely human level to enjoy the good life, like Dives in the Gospel of St. Luke, while someone whom he really cared about — a brother or a sister, say — was living nearly in squalor and destitution. Natural piety would militate against this and sooner or later create an inner pressure which would almost force one to share his wealth — at least in a limited manner — with the needy relative. Otherwise one's love and concern for his needy brother or sister would have to be judged as so much pretence and hypocrisy.

An example comes to mind here of a priest friend of mine who after spending thirteen months as a military chaplain in Korea returned to the "Land of the Great PX" only to discover that he was no longer the same. The raw poverty which he had seen in Korea continued to haunt him until finally he resolved to do something about it. He adopted the habit of making a complete fast one day a week in order, as he put it; "to establish solidarity with the poor of the world." The money saved is given in alms to a relief agency working with the poor in a third world country.

Some seem to think that all that is required to serve the poor is to become poor oneself. One must also *do* something. Christ sent his disciples to the poor not simply to be silent witnesses to poverty but to preach and to heal.

The best way to help a cripple, for example, is not necessarily to break one's own leg and become a cripple oneself. If breaking one's leg renders one ineffective to serve and to help, then to do so would not make much sense. However, more often than not, the contrary is true. Becoming a cripple oneself often renders one's efforts to serve and to redeem more effective, meaningful, and authentic. By voluntarily assuming the condition of the cripple, one ceases to be an outsider. One renounces his citizenship to the world of the healthy and becomes a citizen of the world of the handicapped. He now knows not in theory but by personal experience what it means to be a cripple and he develops a natural sensitivity, empathy, and sixth sense for the problems and needs of the cripple. By the same token, one's service becomes more effective and productive.

In a sense, this is the way Christ went about his mission of serving and redeeming mankind. He voluntarily became a "cripple" himself in order to redeem crippled humanity. In the words of the Epistle to the Hebrews; "Because he himself has suffered and been tempted, he is able to help those who are tempted."

As we have seen in a previous chapter, to a great extent one's surroundings condition one's thinking. Just as day thinking differs from night thinking, so, too, does "rich" thinking differ from "poor" thinking. It is difficult to grasp the mind of the poor while one is living in comfort and ease. By voluntarily throwing one's lot in with the poor, one develops a natural feeling for their problems and thereby becomes able to do more for them.

It is necessary to get in the habit of always looking upon one's possessions in the light of service. Everything I have is not for my own selfish pleasure or satisfaction, but to serve — directly or indirectly — the poor and the hungry of the world. The reason I wish to *have* more is in order to be able to give more. The same holds true for what I *am*: the main reason I wish to *be* more is in order to be able to serve in a more meaningful manner.

In his Letter to the Corinthians St. Paul wrote: "If I give all my goods to the poor and have not charity, it profits me nothing." At first reading this sentence seems puzzling and one can not help but wonder how is it possible to give away one's goods and at the same time offend against charity? It can be done in a number of ways. For example, one could easily give away his goods to satisfy an inner need for personal poverty and by the fact itself reduce his ability to help the needy. In the name of a misguided poverty one could give away all his instruments of service and in so doing sin against a higher, social charity. One could give away his tape recorder (necessary for language study), his camera (needed to take pictures to send to donors in the U.S.), his typewriter (necessary to write begging letters), his jeep (necessary to make effective use of his time), and so on. Here, as in most problems related to poverty and the poor, an important word to keep in mind is the beautiful and thoroughly Christian word "balance."

Another point to consider is the obvious fact that the more one's standard of living resembles that of the people he aspires to serve the more accessible he becomes to them. The hard-core poor are usually victims of a painful inferiority complex. They are at times as sensitive about their social-economic condition as many negroes in the U.S. are about the color of their skin. They are acutely aware of their shabby clothes, unprepossessing appearance, and lack of economic power.

A big expensive-looking rectory with large rooms, shiny floors, and a host of servants running about tends to impress upon the poor the fact of his economic inferiority. It also tends to intimidate him. A pastor who is overly scrubbed, scented, and groomed tends to produce a similar effect. True, the personal warmth of the priest in question can at times dispel these initial impressions; nevertheless, wealth or the appearance of wealth should always be viewed as a barrier rather than a bridge between the heart of the poor and the heart of the priest.

Along these same lines, in *The Decree on the Ministry and Life of the Priests of Vatican II* we read this passage: "Indeed they (priests) are invited to embrace voluntary poverty. By it they will be more clearly likened to Christ and will become more devoted to the sacred ministry. . . . Led, therefore, by the Lord's Spirit who anointed the Savior and sent him to preach the Gospel to the poor, priests as well as bishops will avoid all those things which can offend the poor in any way. More than the other followers of Christ, priests and bishops should spurn any type of vanity in their affairs. Finally, let them have the kind of dwelling which will appear closed to no one and which no one will fear to visit, even the humblest."

If it is easier for the poor to approach a poor priest, the other side of the coin is also true; namely, it is easier for a poor priest to approach the poor than it is for one who is rich. The poor are less ashamed to reveal the ugly wounds of their poverty to a "soul brother" than they are to one who is a total stranger to their world. The doors of their homes and their hearts swing open more readily to a priest who comes from a shack-type rectory, say, than to one who came from a plush, comfortable-looking upper-middle class type of abode.

It is a law of nature that likes attract and dislikes repel. The natural instinct of man is not to love, but to despise, someone who is different than himself, whether the difference be in the area of color, creed, or economic background. The poor, despite all their outward manifestations of respect, are inclined to remain inwardly suspicious and resentful of the rich. At times, they even despise the rich because the presence of his wealth accentuates their own misery and becomes an unconscious source of humiliation. So, too, the poor will normally be suspicious of a priest whose standard of living is markedly higher than their own. As Abbe Pierre, the "ragpicker priest" of Paris, once put it: "To change the rich you must be unlike them. To change the poor you must be like them."

CHAPTER XVIII

Suggestions for the Church of the Poor

In the Gospel of St. Matthew, Christ declared: "Not everyone who says 'Lord, Lord!' will enter the Kingdom of heaven but he who hears the word of God and does it."

From these words we see that Christ had little time for empty speculation, wishful thinking, or mere "notional" assent. Creator of heaven and earth, "in whom all things subsist, are, and have their being," Christ is the source of all reality. He is the supreme realist. As such, his words always contain an implicit call to action, change, and conversion — and this not for some time in the indefinite future but for the immediate now.

With this in mind, I wish to devote the last chapter of this book to practical suggestions on how the ideals of Christian poverty and service of the poor may be translated into action. Accordingly, I have drawn up a list of specific suggestions, which for clarity's sake are divided into five general categories: layman, priest, religious, missioner, and bishop. Ten suggestions are offered for each category, many of which cut across artificial dividing lines and are equally applicable to all the People of God. The fact that the number of suggestions is limited to ten should not be interpreted to mean that they are hard and fast commandments. They are not. They are purely and simply suggestions compiled in order to guide the reader's thinking into the all important area of the quite possible *now*.

Layman

1. Excess fat, which is not the result of illness, should be considered slightly immoral in a lean, hungry, and starving world. If you are overweight (39 million Americans are), resolve to reduce. Give the money saved to the poor of the world.
2. It is estimated that Americans spend 21 billion dollars annually on alcohol and tobacco. Since smoking is a proven health hazard, if you smoke, stop. If you drink to excess, resolve either to cut down or give it up altogether.
3. If you need a new car, buy a less expensive model than you normally would and give the money saved to the poor. Also, the money saved (especially if it is a small foreign car or an American compact) on gasoline and upkeep can be distributed to the poor on a continuing basis.
4. If you are really serious about helping the poor, direct your thoughts away from the old clothes in your attic or the broken toys in your basement. Think rather of reaching into your pocket; think of tightening your belt; think of sacrifice.
5. Get in the habit of thinking poor, living poor, buying poor. For example, instead of butter try using the lower-priced spread. Instead of cream use milk for your coffee. Instead of roast beef eat hamburger occasionally. And so on.
6. When Zacchaeus was converted he said: "Behold, Lord, the half of my goods I give to the poor; and if I have defrauded anyone of anything I restore it fourfold." In this spirit resolve to give the equivalent of one day's pay each month to relieve the insecurity, suffering, and humiliation of Christ present in the poor of the world.
7. Once you resolve to give, do not sound a trumpet to announce the news to the world, but do so with a minimum of fanfare. What is more, do not always look for an emotional return on your charity dollar. For instance, if you are sup-

porting an orphan child in a Vietnamese refugee village, do not insist that she send you a thank you letter each month in English. Such insistence has a way of eating into your charity dollar until little is left to buy food and clothes for the child you are supposed to be helping. Get in the habit of keeping the left hand ignorant of what the right is giving.

8. If there is a death in the family, put the love one to rest with dignity, yes; but above all with simplicity. Leave the four figure satin and mahogany funerals for others who feel the need for such ostentation. In Korea — and most other third world countries — a dead person can be buried with Christian dignity and simplicity for less than $15. It is unseemly and somehow indecent, then, for people in the West to spend 50 or 100 times this amount to put a dead body into the ground.

9. When the subject of foreign aid comes up in conversation, resist the old bromides such as: "The poor you will always have with you," "Am I my brother's keeper?" or "The more we give them the more they hate us!" Instead, generously "support higher taxes so that public authorities can intensify efforts in favor of development. Support higher prices for imported goods so that the producer may be more justly rewarded. And encourage the young to leave their country to serve in developing nations."

10. Petition your parish priest to earmark at least 10% of parish revenue for the poor of the world. Also, if the occasion presents itself, voice opposition to parish building and renovation programs which are not strictly, immediately, and absolutely necessary.

Priests in the U.S.

1. It has been estimated that fifty million dollars was spent in the U.S. in 1968 alone on church renovation. When the occasion presents itself, raise your voice in gentle protest

against this edifice complex which grips the Church and robs it of so much vitality. Urge the Church instead to spend her millions on inner renewal by giving it in alms to the poor of the world.

2. When Simon the magician offered St. Peter money to purchase the Spirit, the Apostle thundered: "May your gold and silver perish with you because you thought you could buy the gift of God with money!" With this in mind, do your part to strike a blow against the abuse of Mass stipends. Instead of putting price tags on Masses and calling them "'free will offerings," why not let the people write their intentions on a slip of paper to be given to the priest and then deposit their offering — amount unspecified — in the parish poor box? Or better yet, why not draw up a plan to eliminate the practice altogether?

3. It has been remarked by people who are in a position to know that kings and princes rarely eat and drink better than the average parish priest. Do not think that your life of voluntary celibacy gives you unlimited license to indulge your appetite for other creature comforts, such as food and drink. To paraphrase the Russian proverb: "Eat bread and salt and speak the truth" of the Gospel.

4. Do not fall victim to the old-age security syndrome and start to accumulate wealth for the rainy day which may never come. Instead, try to strike a happy balance between a minimum of hard-headed provision for the future and a maximum of child-like confidence in God's providence.

5. After the annual retreat each year, go through your personal belongings and eliminate all that is not strictly necessary. Either give it directly to the poor or else sell it and give the proceeds away in alms. Be on your guard against creeping materialism and acquisitiveness which will limit your inner freedom as a priest. A pilgrim prophet of the

eternal should learn to travel light.

6. Try not to make stocks and bonds a way of life, or your own private apostolate. Leave the financial page for the financial wheelers and dealers. Invest any extra funds you may have in eternity by giving them in alms to the poor of the world.

7. Resolve not to purchase personal property for your own pleasure. Once you buy a hunting lodge, a beach house, or a fishing cottage, you will find that maintenance and improvement alone will quickly drain off any and all surplus funds which normally should go to the poor. Along the same lines, resolve not to spend more than $150 on your annual vacation — an amount equivalent to the average annual per capita income in the third world of hunger.

8. Speaking of vacations, leave us not forget that vacation is basically a bourgeois institution accessible only to members of the affluent society. The poor of the world do not even know what the word means. In order to establish solidarity with them cut your normal vacation time in half; use the remaining time to engage in some form of active service of the poor.

9. Poverty means work. An essential part of the spirit of poverty is efficient use of one's time. Some priests bestir themselves a few hours each day and in so doing think they earn their daily steak and apple pie. On the other hand the poor of the world sweat, strain, and break their backs from sun-up to sun-down; and even this is not enough to assure them a full belly. For example, within literally shouting distance of where I am writing these lines, there is a small glass factory which employs 30 boys and girls in their early teens. They work from 7 A.M. to 7 P.M., seven days a week, for a wage of 25¢ a day. This is typical of the treament meted out to the poor of the world. With this in mind ask yourself if your

normal working pace is not just a little too slow, relaxed, or lackadaisical.

10. Make it a policy to contribute at least 10% of parish revenue to the poor — some to the inner-city ghetto dwellers and the rest to the poor of the third world. Make it a rule to open your pulpit more frequently to outside mission and charity appeals. Also, if you yourself cannot go, encourage your brother-priests, who are qualified, to go to Asia, Africa, or Latin America to announce the good news of salvation to the poor.

Priests in Foreign Service on the Missions

1. Do not feel that you are doing your duty simply because the poor in your ear are neither discriminated against nor neglected. This is a negative view of your Gospel-based responsibility. Rather, become aware of the positive priority and privilege of the poor in the Christian scheme of things. Actively seek out the poor with a burning, passionate, prophetic sense of mission.

2. Do not be overly impatient to establish institutions and structures. Rather, try to live among the poor and preach them the good news in a more charismatic manner. Seek to establish a Christian community based on charity and justice, and put off the brick and mortar structuring as long as possible.

3. If a church building is absolutely necessary, see if the people of the parish can not be induced to contribute at least 51% of the construction cost. In this way, even if it is only a barracks, the people of the parish can look at it and say: "It is *our* church."

4. Do not base your criterion of priestly poverty on the standard of living of the native-born priests in your locale. Rather,

adopt an ideal which is more objective and absolute, namely the poverty of Christ as depicted in the Gospels.

5. Do not betray the poverty of Christ in the name of misguided priestly charity. Accordingly, do not be overly concerned about conforming your own personal style of living to that of the priests about you. Be yourself, and be faithful to your own convictions even if they take you outside of the existing current. Even if it means you will be a silent reproach to those who went before you or to those who are working near you.

6. Do not be discouraged if the people of wealth and means in your area refuse to be turned on by your concept of a Church of the poor. Remember that if the message preached ceases to be a scandal and a stumbling block, it is something other than that of Christ.

7. Avoid becoming a commuter-type missioner who must fly home each year to spend a month with his family. Avoid becoming a tourist-type missioner who, armed with camera guide-book, is off and traveling at every pretext. Avoid becoming a dilettante-type of missioner who likes to dabble in the culture of the rich and middle-class of his adopted land but who remains completely ignorant of the subculture of its slums and ghettos.

8. Do not seek peace at any price. For fear of rocking the boat, do not remain silent about injustice to the poor, even if the injustice is committed by the powers that are in the Church. Christ came to cast fire on the earth, and the fire of which he speaks is, primarily, justice.

9. Since the foremost preoccupation of the poor of every time and every place is what they eat, priestly poverty should find some expression in this area also. A well-balanced diet and simplicity of style are not necessarily opposed. While eating wholesome nourishing food, take care that you are

not a source of scandal to the poor who work in your kitchen.

10. Remember that for Christian poverty to be complete, it must include four elements. It must be both spiritual, and material. It must be closely joined to prayer; and it must in some way be related to service of the poor.

Religious

1. Some religious seem determined to be poor no matter what the cost. They go to great expense to procure specially-made sandals, mantles, and the like, because this is what their founder judged to be an expression of poverty three or four hundred years ago. Try to forget about the practice of anachronistic religious poverty and concentrate more on common sense, twentieth-century *poor-man* poverty.

2. Do not look upon every financial windfall as the direct result of divine intervention in the course of human events. Have the courage to look every gift horse carefully in the mouth, and on occasion, even refuse it.

3. When you show visitors around your new one million, or three million, or six million dollar motherhouse, try to refrain repeating such phrases as, "God has been so good to us," or "Thanks to St. Joseph we have been able to finance this beautiful building!" Although the words may be intended to edify, in the context they may elicit an opposite reaction. Don't blame God, or St. Joseph, for your wealth and expensive taste. Rather be honest, and humbly take the blame yourself.

4. Don't try to defend the luxurious food on your table in the name of economy by stating that what is spent on nutrition is saved on doctors' bills. If you write to the Department of Agriculture in Washington they will show you how a perfectly balanced and nutritious — although not the most tasty — diet can be provided for less than a dollar a day.

5. Ask yourself in all sincerity, is the magazine which you

publish really necessary? Or is it simply an expression of a collective desire for prestige? Also ask yourself, are your fund-raising appeals really honest? Do you devote 90% of coverage to the 5% of your personnel who are serving overseas because this is what sells? Do you collect money in the name of the poor to build up a congregation of the rich?

6. In his entire lifetime, Jesus never traveled more than 200 or 300 miles from the place where he was born. The poor of the world are rarely permitted the luxury of traveling even a hundred miles from the place where they see the light of day. When the next time comes for you to travel, ask yourself the question: Is this trip really necessary?

7. Don't spend too much time and effort cultivating the financial, political and intellectual elite. This elite has often proven illusory and, at times, has done more harm than good to the Church. Concentrate rather on serving the poor — the only true "elite" in the Christian scheme of things.

8. Remember that insecurity is an essential ingredient of poor man poverty and taking a risk is an inherent part of Christianity. Do not aspire to a bourgeois apostolate or a worryless type of poverty. Learn how to be psychologically comfortable in the uncertain, the insecure, and the unknown and you will be amazed at how easy it becomes to penetrate the hearts of the poor.

9. If you are a superior burdened with the responsibility of building something for the community, do not feel obliged to design something with the comfort and pleasure of the weakest member in view. Do not betray Gospel simplicity out of fear of the complaints and criticism of those under you. At times you do them an injustice by thinking that they will be dissatisfied with anything less than a new Hotel Hilton.

10. Resolve to give at least 10% of your collective wealth, in area of both money and personnel, to the poor of the third world of Asia, Africa, and Latin America.

Bishops

1. "I don't want to be a millionaire, I just want to *live* like one," said the jolly American bishop in jest. The unfunny fact, however, is that many bishops *do* live like millionaires. They eat like them, dress like them, travel like them, and live in houses like them. Resolve to be a bishop after the mind of St. Paul who worked with his hands and knew the meaning of poverty, insecurity, and hunger.

2. Do not be reluctant to receive a fellow bishop from a third world country who comes to you for a handout. Also realize that when you begin to speak of your own poverty to such a one your words will inevitably sound unconvincing. The fact that your diocese has a debt of five million dollars, say, does not necessarily mean that it is destitute. *Everybody* in America is in debt paying off his home, his car, or his furniture simply because credit is part and parcel of the American scene.

3. Resolve to give up the practice of "spiritual birth control" in the area of vocations. Realize that a vocation is not your property but God's. Open wide the doors of your diocese to all outside vocation directors, especially if they are looking for men to announce the good news to the poor.

4. Don't discourage your seminarians or young priests from going to the missions. Don't ask them to wait three, five, or ten years. Instead, generously adhere to the *Decree on the Missionary Activity of the Church* which states the following: "The bishop will also gladly foster vocations to mission communities among young people and clerics. He will react with a grateful spirit if God should call some of them to engage in the missionary activity of the Church" (38).

5. For every trip you make to Europe, resolve to make at least one to a third world country. See for yourself, on a regular basis, how the Other Half lives and your life will no longer

be the same.
6. A *suggestion* for *future* bishops. When your episcopal nomination comes through, resolve to forego the customary post-consecration celebration which often runs into four and five figures. Rather break the bread of rejoicing in utmost simplicity, and give the money saved to the poor of the world.
7. Think about the possibility of moving your episcopal residence from the suburban area where it is now probably located to an inner-city parish rectory, or maybe even to a lower middle-class apartment.
8. Drop your membership in the local country club. Forego the company of the butter and eggs set and try to get closer to the common people.
9. Realize that the Church of the future is unquestionably a Church of the poor. Accordingly, approve construction of only strictly necessary church buildings in your diocese and see to it that even these be simple, austere, and completely functional.
10. Resolve to contribute at least 10% of all diocesan revenue in alms to the poor of the world and encourage 10% of your diocesan priests to serve on the missions at least for a time.

I wish to end this invitation-to-action chapter by calling to mind the beautiful words of Cardinal Newman: "Therein lies the nobility of faith that we have the heart to dare something." Our times call for bold action, striking out in new directions, and the running of risks. Nothing is more bold, daring, or risky than a really serious attempt to imitate the poor Christ of the Gospels no matter what the cost, no matter what the consequences. At the same time one must never lose sight of the fact that a life of poverty and service is intended to be a life of joy. If it is the real thing and not just ersatz, it must be lived from day to day with a certain light-hearted, child-of-God, Christian gusto.